A Taste Of Montana

MW00907431

A Collection of Our Best Recipes

To Deb ~
Hope you enjoy this book —
Much love —
Mary Laylin

Montana
Bed & Breakfast Association

Edited By Tracy & Phyllis Winters

Winters Publishing
P.O. Box 501
Greensburg, Indiana   47240

800-457-3230
812-663-4948

Front cover photo © 1999 John Reddy
Courtesy of: The Sanders - Helena's Bed & Breakfast
                Helena, Montana

The information about the inns and the recipes were supplied by the inns
themselves. The rate information was current at the time of submission,
but is subject to change. Every effort has been made to assure that the book
is accurate. Neither the editors, The Montana Bed & Breakfast Association,
the individual inns nor the publisher assume responsibility for any errors,
whether typographical or otherwise.

Library of Congress Card Catalog Number 99-90557
ISBN 1-883651-11-5

A Note From The President

Welcome to a culinary journey through the Big Sky country of Montana. The Montana Bed and Breakfast Association guides you along in *A Taste Of Montana*. Montana's elite group of Bed and Breakfasts have joined together to offer up some of their most sought-after recipes. Every day, all over the state, our guests are requesting the recipe for that delicious gourmet delight they just enjoyed. I can't count the number of times we've sent treats out the door with them, as they continue their travels through this beautiful state.

Bed and Breakfast innkeepers are well known far and wide for their culinary skills. Why not put together a cookbook from the best cooks in the state? We found prying those recipes out of the innkeepers to be quite a chore. It's difficult to give out those secrets that make you special. We played on their pride of "Being the Best in the Last Best Place". If we were to put together a cookbook, it had better be the best!

We have achieved our goal. *A Taste Of Montana* is a collection of some of the most mouth-watering culinary treats to be found. The Montana Bed and Breakfast Association members have outdone themselves in this joint effort. There is only one way to get more pleasure from this cookbook. Stay at one of these Bed and Breakfasts and experience the famed "Montana Hospitality" for yourself.

CONTENTS

CONTENTS

Rates

We have used the following symbols to represent the price range of the Bed & Breakfast Inns:

$ - $50 or less
$$ - $51 to $75
$$$ - $76 to $100
$$$$ - more than $100

Please call ahead to verify rates and room availability.

Appleton Inn Bed & Breakfast

1999 Euclid Avenue • Helena, MT 59601
406-449-7492 800-956-1999
Web site: www.appletoninn.com
E-mail: appleton@ixi.net
Innkeepers: Cheryl Boid and Tom Woodall

Relax in the splendor of Helena's Victorian Inn built in 1890 by George Appleton and listed on the National Historic Register. Adorned in original oak and cherry hardwoods, *Appleton Inn* offers five spacious, individually-decorated guest rooms complete with antiques and hand-crafted furnishings, private in-room bath, television, telephone, and all modern comforts. A Family Suite is also available. *Appleton Inn* has been awarded 3 diamonds by AAA and 3 crowns by ABBA. Enjoy afternoon refreshments in the parlor or perennial gardens while planning activities for the evening in this wonderfully historic city. Return to the *Inn* for a relaxing cup of tea, curl up with a good book or take a long soak in a clawfoot bathtub. After a well-rested sleep, converse with newfound friends over a delicious full breakfast served on original antique Franciscan Appleware and fine linens, making any morning in Montana special.

Rates: $$$ Includes full breakfast. Children are welcome. Pets allowed with prior approval. Restricted smoking. We accept MasterCard, Visa, Am Ex and Discover.

HUCKLEBERRY BLINTZ

1 cup milk	1 cup fresh huckleberries
3/4 cup flour	or blueberries
3 eggs	Vanilla yogurt & fresh
2 tablespoons oil	berries for garnish
Pinch of salt	

In blender add milk, flour, eggs, oil and salt. Blend to a heavy cream consistency. Remove lid and let it rest for 20 minutes. Spray a hot griddle with cooking spray. Measure 1/4 cup batter and spread out thinly to form a crepe. Cook until firm, turn over to slightly brown, turn back over and spoon a row of huckleberries off-center. Quickly roll up the crepe, set it to the side of the griddle, turning occasionally until lightly browned. Repeat with remainder of batter. Can also be placed in warm oven until all crepes are made. Serve three crepes to a plate, topped with vanilla yogurt and fresh berries. Makes 10 crepes.

WILD RICE QUICHE

1 cup wild rice cooked with finely chopped onion, carrots & celery	8 eggs
	3/4 cup half and half
	1/2 teaspoon salt
1/3 cup diced, fully-cooked ham	1/4 teaspoon pepper
	1/2 teaspoon dried
1 cup shredded Monterey Jack cheese	tarragon
	1 teaspoon dried parsley

Cook wild rice with finely chopped onion, carrots and celery, to taste, until done. Spray a 9" deep-dish pie plate with cooking spray. Place rice, ham and cheese in bottom of pie plate. In medium bowl beat the eggs. Add half and half, salt, pepper and tarragon. Pour over mixture in pie plate. Sprinkle parsley over the pie. Bake at 350° for 45 minutes or until the center is set. Makes 6 servings.

The Barrister Bed & Breakfast

416 North Ewing Street • Helena, MT 59601
406-443-2330
Innkeepers: Nick Jacques and Yvette McCormack

The Barrister is an elegant 1880 Victorian three-story mansion listed on the National Register of Historic Places. It is adjacent to the magnificent St. Helena Cathedral and walking distance to downtown's fine restaurants, shops and galleries. The mansion features six ornate fireplaces, original stained glass windows, high ceilings and carved staircases. Five guest rooms on the second floor are exquisitely decorated, have private baths and feature queen size turn-of-the-century replica beds. The first floor common area boasts a formal dining room, grand piano and guitar in the parlor, enclosed sun porch with ice cream parlor tables, business center/game room, office with computer and office equipment, large outside porch and large yard for guests' use and enjoyment. Located in the center of Helena, with airport shuttle and evening refreshments.

Rates: $$$ Includes full breakfast. Children are welcome. Pets are allowed. Smoking is restricted to outside porches, please. We accept MasterCard, Visa and Am Ex.

BANANA PECAN PANCAKES

1 cup all purpose flour
1 cup whole wheat flour
2 tablespoons sugar
2 teaspoons baking
  powder
1 teaspoon baking soda
1/2 teaspoon salt
2 1/2 cups buttermilk

2 tablespoons vegetable
  oil
1 teaspoon vanilla extract
2 eggs
2 - 3 bananas, sliced into
  1/4" rounds
6 tablespoons chopped
  pecans

Combine dry ingredients in large bowl; stir well. Combine buttermilk, oil, vanilla and eggs in small bowl; stir well. Add to flour mixture, stirring until smooth. Spoon about 1/3 cup batter for each pancake onto hot griddle sprayed with Pam. Lay banana rounds on top of pancakes, sprinkle with pecans. Turn when tops are covered with bubbles and edges are cooked. Serve with Cinnamon Syrup and sprinkle with pecans. Makes 6 servings of 3 pancakes per serving.

CINNAMON SYRUP

1 cup light corn syrup
2/3 cup honey
1/4 cup water

1/2 teaspoon ground
  cinnamon
1/2 cup evaporated milk

Mix all ingredients, except evaporated milk, in medium saucepan. Boil for two minutes, cool for five minutes. Stir in evaporated milk. Makes enough to top about 20 pancakes.

Big Creek Pines Bed & Breakfast

2986 Highway 93 North • Stevensville, MT 59870
406-642-6475
Web site: www.wtp.net/go/bigcreek
E-mail: bcp1@cybernet1.com
Innkeepers: Rosemary and Joe Beason

Imagine fresh flowers, morning sun, birds singing, deer grazing, a flowing creek, majestic mountain views, and you are at *Big Creek Pines*. Our breakfast is prepared for you to savor and enjoy. Freshly baked breads hot from the oven accompany a variety of delectable entrees, along with a variety of fresh fruit and juice smoothies. Breakfast is served in the great room by the fire or on warm summer mornings on the covered veranda, where you can listen to the birds sing, overlooking creek, meadow and mountains. Four spacious immaculate and individually-appointed guest rooms boast private in-room baths. Attention to detail was given when decorating, with family mementos making the inn warm and inviting. We are located just twenty-seven miles south of Missoula where Montana began, and where Lewis & Clark's expedition passed through in 1805. Be sure to bring your hiking boots, fishing rods, binoculars and camera and check out our web site.

Rates: $$ - $$$ Includes full breakfast. Cannot accommodate pets. Restricted smoking. We accept MasterCard, Visa, checks and cash.

❖ *Recipes From Big Creek Pines Bed & Breakfast* ❖

APPLE TATIN

1 sheet puff pastry
3 tablespoons softened
butter
2 Granny Smith apples,
peeled, cored, thinly
sliced

Lemon juice, as
needed
1 teaspoon lemon
zest
1/4 cup sugar

Arrange pastry in either a 10" tart pan or 6 small individual tart pans. Spread pastry with 1 tablespoon butter. Toss apples in lemon juice, and arrange the slices attractively on the pastry. Sprinkle with the lemon zest and sugar, dot with remaining butter. Bake at 425° for 20 - 25 minutes or until golden brown. Serve warm. Makes 8 servings.

BIG CREEK PINES BREAKFAST PIE

2 tablespoons olive oil
1/2 teaspoon garlic
powder
Baguette bread, sliced
1/4" thick
1 cup provolone cheese,
shredded
2/3 cup milk
2 teaspoons flour
1 (3-ounce) pkg.
cream cheese
1 teaspoon chopped
chives

Salt & pepper, to
taste
1 tablespoon snipped
basil
8 eggs, beaten
2 tablespoons milk
Pinch of salt
2 tablespoons butter
1/2 cup chopped ham or
bacon, cooked
2 chopped tomatoes and
fresh herbs for
garnish

Spritz a 9" pie plate with oil. Brush cut baguette slices (enough to cover bottom and sides of pie plate) with oil; sprinkle with garlic powder. Arrange bread in pie plate and bake uncovered at 400° for 8 minutes. Sprinkle with 1/2 cup shredded cheese, return to oven and bake just until cheese is melted. In medium saucepan stir together 2/3 cup milk and flour. Stir in cream cheese, chives, salt, pepper and basil. Cook and stir until thickened. Beat together eggs, 2 tablespoons milk and salt. In large skillet melt butter, pour in egg mixture. Cook just until mixture begins to set on bottom. Using spatula, lift and fold partially cooked eggs so uncooked portion flows underneath. Cook eggs throughout but still moist. Fold in cream cheese, chives and meat. Spoon egg mixture into crust and sprinkle with remaining shredded cheese. Bake at 350° for approximately 15 minutes until heated through. Sprinkle pie with chopped tomatoes and herbs. Cut into wedges to serve. Makes 6 servings.

BREAKFAST CRANAPPLE PUDDING

1/2 cup butter	2 tablespoons baking
2 cups sugar	soda
2 large eggs	2 teaspoons cinnamon
6 cups grated Granny	3/4 teaspoon nutmeg
Smith apples	1/2 teaspoon cloves
1 cup + 2 tablespoons	1 cup cranberries, cut
all purpose flour	into halves
2/3 cup whole wheat flour	1/2 cup chopped nuts

Preheat oven to 350°. In large bowl cream butter, sugar and eggs until fluffy. Stir in apples. Sift together flours, baking soda, cinnamon, nutmeg and cloves. Add to creamed mixture and mix well. Fold in cranberries and nuts. Pour mixture into an oil-spritzed 9" x 13" glass baking dish; bake for approximately 40 - 45 minutes. Cut into serving pieces. Serve with a dollop of vanilla yogurt, a fresh mint leaf and sugar dipped cranberry on top. Makes 12 - 15 servings.

POACHED PEARS WITH STRAWBERRY COULIS

4 pears, peeled, cored	Coulis:
from the bottom leaving	1/2 cup strawberry jelly
stem attached	2 tablespoons orange
3/4 cup orange juice	juice
1 tablespoon lemon juice	Mint leaf for garnish

Heat pears, 3/4 cup orange juice and lemon juice in saucepan. Cover and simmer approximately 15 minutes, or until tender. Transfer pears and poaching liquid to bowl; cover and refrigerate. Melt jelly and 2 tablespoons orange juice in saucepan. To serve: Divide coulis onto individual serving dishes. Stand pear upright on top; drizzle pear with small amount of coulis, add a mint leaf by the stem, and serve. Makes 4 servings.

MERRY BERRY COMPOTE

1 cup frozen strawberries
1 cup frozen raspberries
1 cup blueberries
1 cup blackberries
1 cup water

1 cup honey
1 tablespoon chopped fresh mint
Fresh mint leaves for garnish

Combine all fruit, water and honey in saucepan. Bring to a boil, reduce heat and simmer for 10 - 15 minutes. Remove from heat, stir in mint. To serve, put in pretty compote and garnish with fresh mint leaves. Serve with your favorite breakfast entree. Variations: Prior to simmering add 1/4 cup butter, then thicken with a bit of cornstarch, to serve over your favorite waffle recipe. Also wonderful served warm over vanilla ice cream. Makes 4 - 6 servings.

ROSEMARY'S BREAKFAST FOCACCIA

1 pkg. active dry yeast
1 cup warm water
2 tablespoons canola oil
1/2 teaspoon salt
3 to 3 1/4 cups all purpose flour
2 tablespoons melted butter

3 tablespoons granulated sugar
1/2 teaspoon cinnamon
1/4 cup chopped nuts
1/2 cup sifted powdered sugar
1 tablespoon light cream
Few drops almond flavoring

In large bowl dissolve yeast in warm water. Add oil, salt and flour. Mix well and knead to make smooth, moderately stiff dough, adding more flour if necessary. Shape into ball and place in greased bowl, turning to grease surface. Cover and let rise in warm place until double, for approximately one hour. Punch dough down, divide in half, cover, and let rest for 10 minutes. Grease a 12" pizza pan. Press dough into pan and prick surface with a fork. Brush with melted butter. In small bowl combine granulated sugar and cinnamon; sprinkle this and nuts over dough. Let rise for 15 - 20 minutes and bake for 20 - 25 minutes in preheated 350° oven until lightly browned. While focaccia is baking, combine powdered sugar, cream and almond flavoring. Drizzle with icing while focaccia is still warm. Serve warm. Makes 8 - 10 servings.

Big Horn Bed & Breakfast

Box 9 - 33 Lower Rock Creek Road • Philipsburg, MT 59858
406-859-3109
Web site: www.bighornmontana.com
E-mail: phl3109@montana.com
Innkeepers: Virginia and Jerry Gallagher

The Big Horn extends a hearty welcome to all our guests. Nestled in a mountain setting on a blue-ribbon trout stream 15 miles west of Philipsburg, our log home features a large living and dining area with fireplace and decks. We have two beautiful guest rooms - Devon and Ashley - with a shared bath. And we use only environmentally friendly products by Melaleuca for your comfort and safety. If you're searching for serene mountain beauty with a touch of natural elegance, where big horn sheep roam the hills and eagles soar the Montana skies to the music of bluebirds and other wildlife, we have a place for you. Why Rock Creek? It's beautiful, it's peaceful and the fishing is great.

Rates: $$ Includes full breakfast. Children are welcome. No pets or smoking, please. We accept MasterCard and Visa.

CHOCOLATE CHIP TREASURE COOKIES

1 1/2 cups graham cracker crumbs
1/2 cup flour
2 teaspoons baking powder
1 (14-ounce) can Eagle brand sweetened condensed milk

1/2 cup margarine or butter (softened)
1 1/2 cups flaked coconut
2 cups semi-sweet chocolate chips
1 cup chopped walnuts

Preheat oven to 350°. In small bowl mix graham cracker crumbs, flour and baking powder. Add sweetened condensed milk and butter, mix well. Stir in coconut, chocolate chips and walnuts. Drop by rounded tablespoons onto greased cookie sheets. Bake 9 - 10 minutes or until lightly browned. Store loosely covered at room temperature. Recipe may be doubled. Makes 2 1/2 dozen cookies.

HAMBURGER CASSEROLE

6 or 7 sliced potatoes
1 pound hamburger, browned and drained
1 can cream of chicken soup

1 soup can water
1 cup mozzarella cheese

Slice potatoes and place in large casserole dish. Brown hamburger, drain, and spread on top of potatoes. Mix soup and water together in saucepan and bring to a boil. Pour over meat and potatoes. Sprinkle cheese on top. Bake at 350° for one hour, or until potatoes are done and cheese is lightly browned. Makes 6 servings.

Birdseye Bed & Breakfast

6890 Raven Road • Helena, MT 59602
406-449-4380
Web site: birdseyebb.com
E-mail: rooms@birdseyebb.com
Innkeeper: Rob Morris

When is the last time you sat on a bale of hay ... or entered a hen house to gather warm, fresh eggs? Have you ever petted a llama or allowed a billy goat with 2-foot horns to eat from your hand? You can experience all this ... and more. Sit on the porch and count the endless chain of mountain ranges that form a backdrop for the grazing llamas and angora goats. *Birdseye B&B* is located 8 miles from Helena and 2 miles up a mountain road. We offer five rooms with comfortable beds for your guaranteed rest and a view from the bedroom "that'll knock your socks off!" Come morning, enjoy those hand-picked eggs, along with some homemade goodies for a hearty country breakfast. Grab your coffee cup and "schmooze" the art gallery where you'll find fine art by Montana artists. Host Rob, artist and sculptor, invites you to visit his studio.

Rates: $$ - $$$ Includes full breakfast. Children are welcome.
Restricted smoking. We accept MasterCard and Visa.

PEACH BIRDSEYE

1 cookie (favorite variety)	Cool Whip, to taste
1 scoop French vanilla	4 slices of peaches
ice cream	Raspberry syrup

Place cookie in small bowl. Add ice cream on top of cookie. Place a little roll of Cool Whip with edge of spoon at 12:00, 3:00, 6:00 and 9:00 around ice cream. Place peach slices between dollops of Cool Whip. Start at center and swirl on raspberry syrup in a clockwise direction. Makes 1 serving.

RECIPE FOR A HAPPY MARRIAGE

1 cup of consideration	1 reasonable budget
1 cup of courtesy	A generous dash of cooperation
2 cupfuls of flattery (carefully concealed)	3 teaspoons of pure extract of "I'm sorry"
2 cupfuls milk of human kindness	1 cup contentment
1 gallon faith in God and each other	2 children (at least)
2 cupfuls of praise	1 romantic getaway a month (at least)
1 small pinch of in-laws	

Mix all together, flavor with frequent portions of recreation and a dash of happy memories. Stir well and remove any specks of jealousy, temper or criticism. Sweeten well with generous portions of love, and keep warm with a steady flame of devotion. Never serve with a cold shoulder or a hot tongue. Yield: 1 happy marriage.

The Bungalow Bed & Breakfast

2020 Highway 287 - P.O. Box 168 • Wolf Creek, MT 59648
406-235-4276
E-mail: bngalow@aol.com
Innkeeper: Pat O'Connell Anderson

The Bungalow is a red cedar log lodge built in 1911 by early day
Montana entrepreneur C. B. Power. The architect, Robert Reamer,
also built lodges in Yellowstone Park. It is on the National Register
of Historic Places and has been in the innkeeper's family since 1946.
Located under a magnificent rock reef not far from beautiful Wolf
Creek Canyon and I-15, it is close to blue ribbon fly fishing on the
Missouri and Dearborn Rivers as well as a scenic boat trip along the
Lewis and Clark Trail. Enjoy the quiet of nature and watch the deer
meander through the yard or gaze up at the eagles soaring overhead.
Spend an enjoyable evening in the great room in front of the massive
stone fireplace, and wake to a full gourmet breakfast served in the
formal dining room. We offer four guest rooms. Conveniently
located off scenic Highway 287. Enjoy great western hospitality!

*Rates: $$$ Includes full breakfast. Children are welcome. No pets,
please. Restricted smoking.*

FRESH HERB FRITTATA

1 tablespoon margarine
   or butter
1/2 cup chopped red
   onion
6 medium mushrooms,
   cleaned and sliced
1/2 cup chopped spinach
   (frozen or fresh)
Diced meat, if desired

8 large eggs
1/4 cup milk
Chopped fresh herbs, to
   taste (sweet basil,
   rosemary, marjoram,
   parsley, etc.)
Finely grated cheese &
   fresh basil leaves for
   garnish

Melt butter or margarine in 10" - 12" ovenproof skillet; sauté onions and mushrooms slightly, and stir in spinach. Add meat at this point if desired. Beat eggs and milk; pour slowly over vegetable mixture over medium heat. Cook slowly until mixture begins to set. Sprinkle with fine herbs on top and bake at 400° until set, about 15 minutes. Garnish with a small amount of finely grated cheese and fresh basil leaves. Cut into wedges and serve. Makes 4 - 6 servings.

HONEY OATMEAL BREAD

2 pkgs. yeast
1/2 cup warm water
2 1/2 cups scalded milk
1/2 cup honey
6 tablespoons butter or
   margarine

2 1/2 teaspoons salt
3 cups white flour
3 1/2 cups whole wheat
   flour
2 cups oatmeal
Melted butter for tops

Dissolve yeast in water. In large bowl, pour milk over honey, butter and salt. Cool to lukewarm. Add 2 cups flour, oats and yeast mixture. Mix well. Add additional flour to make a soft dough. Turn out onto floured surface and knead until elastic. Shape dough into a ball and place in greased bowl, turning to coat. Cover and let rise until double, about one hour. Punch down, let rest for 10 minutes. Shape into 2 loaves and place in greased pans. Brush with melted butter. Cover and let rise for 45 minutes. Bake at 350° for 45 minutes.

GINGER PANCAKES WITH LEMON SAUCE

Pancakes:
4 cups whole wheat
  pancake mix
3 teaspoons ginger
2 teaspoons
  cinnamon
1/2 teaspoon nutmeg
1/2 teaspoon cloves
3 1/2 cups water
2 tablespoons molasses

Lemon Sauce:
1 cup sugar
2 1/2 tablespoons
  cornstarch
2 cups water
4 tablespoons butter or
  margarine
Grated rind, juice and
  pulp of 2 large lemons

Before cooking pancakes, prepare Lemon Sauce: Mix sugar and cornstarch, and stir in water gradually in medium saucepan. Bring to a boil over medium heat, stirring constantly, for about five minutes or until thick. Remove from heat and stir in butter, juice and lemon rind. Blend all pancake ingredients until smooth, adding water to desired consistency. Cook on lightly greased or sprayed griddle until golden brown. Serve sauce over pancakes. Makes 4 - 6 servings.

PAT'S BREAKFAST STRATA

8 - 10 ounces turkey
  sausage, browned &
  crumbled
10 - 12 slices bread
1/2 pkg. frozen chopped
  spinach, partially
  thawed
2 cups grated medium
  cheddar cheese

3 eggs, beaten
1 1/2+ cups milk
1 1/2 teaspoons dry
  mustard
1 can cream of mushroom
  soup
1/2 soup can milk
Chopped tomatoes or
  salsa for garnish

Spray six (12-ounce) ramekins with non-stick coating. Brown sausage, breaking up into small pieces. Cube bread and layer in bottom of ramekins. Top with sausage, chopped spinach and cheese. Mix eggs, and enough milk to have 3 cups of egg/milk mixture with dry mustard and pour 1/2 cup of this mixture over each dish. Cover and refrigerate overnight. In the morning, mix soup with half a soup can of milk and spoon over casseroles. Top with tomatoes or salsa and bake at 350° for 30 - 40 minutes. Makes 6 servings.

❖ *Recipes From The Bungalow Bed & Breakfast* ❖

PEACH MELBA FRENCH TOAST

2 loaves French bread
6 eggs
2 tablespoons vanilla
3 tablespoons sugar

2 teaspoons cinnamon
2 cups milk
3 - 4 fresh peaches,
   sliced

Filling:
1/2 - 3/4 cup softened
   cream cheese

2 - 3 tablespoons seedless
   raspberry jam

Mix together filling ingredients. Cut French bread into 1" slices with a pocket at 1/2" extending almost to the bottom. Spread cream cheese and jam mixture in pocket. Mix eggs, vanilla, sugar, cinnamon and milk and beat well. Dip each piece of bread in egg mixture and cook on lightly sprayed or greased griddle or pan at medium heat until lightly browned on both sides. While bread is cooking, slice peaches into saucepan. Sprinkle with ascorbic acid or Fruit Fresh and heat just until juices are released. Stir in a few fresh raspberries & spoon over French toast. Lightly dust with powdered sugar. Makes 8 servings.

THE BUNGALOW'S IRISH PASTIES

1 round steak, trimmed
   well and diced
4 - 6 potatoes, peeled
   and cubed
2 - 3 carrots, peeled
   and shredded

1 - 2 onions, chopped
Salt & pepper, to taste
Butter
Milk
Prepared pie pastry for
   3 double-crust pies

Dice round steak and potatoes into 1/3" - 1/2" pieces. Place potatoes in salted water as you work to keep them from discoloring. Mix meat and vegetables together in large bowl and season with salt and pepper to taste. Roll out pastry into 6 or 8 circles. Salt and pepper surface of pastry and divide meat mixture equally and place on half the pastry circle. Dot each mixture with 1/2 tablespoon butter; fold pastry over meat mixture and seal edges. Make 3 - 4 small vent slits in top. Place on lightly greased or sprayed cookie sheet with edges or jelly roll pan. Brush with milk and bake at 350° for one hour, or until golden brown. Serve with beef gravy or desired condiments. Makes 6 - 8 servings.

Carriage House Ranch

P.O. Box 1249 • Big Timber, MT 59011-1249
406-932-5339
E-mail: carriagehouse@mcn.net
Innkeepers: John Haller and Sally DeStefano

The Carriage House Ranch B&B is in the heart of Horse Whisperer Country on 680 acres of rolling ranch land, surrounded by the legendary Crazy Mountains (almost in the back yard!) and the Beartooth Mountains in the distance. Big Timber Creek runs through the property, only 7 miles from fishing thrills provided by the Yellowstone and Boulder Rivers. Deer, antelope and an occasional bear roam the ranch. The historic creekside 3-bedroom Carriage House was built in 1910. The new 3-bedroom ranch house features mountain view guest rooms, and the equestrian center sponsors riding instruction and events. Anyone seeking the ultimate get-away will love *Carriage House Ranch*. Full breakfast. Lunch and dinner available. Convenient to Bozeman, Billings and Yellowstone.

Rates: $$$$ Includes full breakfast. Children over age 10 are welcome. Pets are allowed. Restricted smoking. We accept MasterCard and Visa.

WILD EGGS

1 cup uncooked wild rice
1/4 cup butter
1/2 cup water chestnuts
2 tablespoons chives
8 ounces mushrooms

3 cups chicken broth
6 - 8 large eggs, poached
 or fried
Orange slices and herbs
 for garnish

Wash rice. Melt butter, then add rice, water chestnuts, chives and mushrooms. Cook and stir for about 20 minutes. Heat oven to 325°. Pour rice mixture into ungreased 1 1/2 quart casserole. Heat broth to boiling, stir into rice mixture. Cover lightly. Bake for 1 1/2 hours, until all liquid is absorbed and rice is tender and fluffy. (Rice can be reheated easily in microwave oven.) Top plated rice with a poached or fried egg. Garnish with orange slices and parsley or fresh basil. Makes 6 - 8 servings.

WINTER TOMATO SOUP

1/2 cup chopped celery
2 tablespoons butter or
 bacon drippings
1 (16-ounce) can stewed
 tomatoes
1 (10 1/2-ounce) can
 condensed consommé
 or chicken broth

1/2 cup dry white wine
3 tablespoons chopped
 green onions
1 tablespoon lemon juice
1 tablespoon cornstarch
1/2 cup water
Dash of curry
Cheese croutons/garnish

Sauté the celery in butter or bacon drippings until soft, for about five minutes, over medium heat. Add tomatoes, consommé, wine, onions, lemon juice and cornstarch blended with water. Blend well. Add curry. Simmer for 15 - 20 minutes, stirring occasionally. Garnish with cheese croutons. Makes 4 servings.

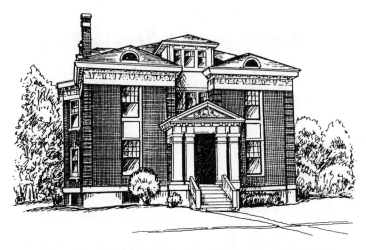

Charley Montana Bed & Breakfast

103 North Douglas • Glendive, MT 59330
888-395-3207
Web site: http://www.wtp.net/go/charley.html
E-mail: charley@midrivers.com
Innkeepers: Jim and Katherine Lee

Live like a turn-of-the-century cattle baron at *Charley Montana Bed & Breakfast*. Charles Krug built this 8,000 square foot home, known locally as the Krug Mansion, in 1907. The architecturally significant building is on the National Register of Historic Places, and is one of Eastern Montana's treasures. Original woodwork gleams; leaded glass sheds rainbows. Visitors are invited to view and use Krug family heirlooms, and read from the extensive collection of antique books and historic western reading. Guests choose from seven comfortable air-conditioned rooms, with queen or twin beds; five rooms have private baths. The Yellowstone River and historic Bell Street Bridge are just outside the back door. Glendive, Montana is scenic, historic and conveniently located on I-94. Visit Makoshika State Park's spectacular badlands and dinosaur digs. Stroll to restaurants, casinos and shops. Stop on your way to Yellowstone, Glacier or Teddy Roosevelt parks, or the Lewis & Clark interpretive center.

Rates: $$ Includes full breakfast. Children are welcome. No pets or smoking, please.

RANCH COOK ANNIE KRUG'S FAMOUS GOULASH

2 pounds good ground beef
1/4 cup Crisco
2 large bunches celery, cut fine
5 large onions, cut fine
3 tablespoons salt (yes, folks, that's the authentic recipe!)
1 teaspoon black pepper
1 large can tomatoes
1 can tomato soup

3 tablespoons broken spaghetti (it's in there as thickening)
2 peppers, one red and one green, chopped
1 green pimento (or 1 jar red pimento)
1/2 cup butter
Chili powder the size of two kidney beans
2 large cans kidney beans

Toss beef in frying pan for 15 minutes, adding Crisco the last 5 minutes. Add celery, onions, salt, pepper, tomatoes, soup, spaghetti, peppers, pimento and butter. Pour into casserole. Bake at 350° for 45 minutes. Add chili powder and kidney beans the last 20 minutes. Serve over baked or boiled potatoes, or hot biscuits. This heritage recipe makes 20 servings.

OLD-FASHIONED POTATO PANCAKES

4 cups peeled, diced, raw baking potatoes
2 tablespoons all purpose flour
1/2 teaspoon baking powder

1/4 teaspoon baking soda
1/2 teaspoon salt
2 eggs
2 tablespoons Butter Flavor Crisco

Using blender or food processor, liquefy 3 1/2 cups of potatoes. Blend in the dry ingredients and eggs. Add the remaining 1/2 cup potatoes, blending or processing until chunks are quite small. Cook in Crisco on 375° griddle until crispy outside, tender inside, turning once. Serves 6 big appetites. We serve with a heap of rustic bacon, grilled tart apples, and a fruity syrup, sometimes our own homemade chokecherry compote.

Coleman-Fee Mansion Bed & Breakfast

500 Missouri Avenue • Deer Lodge, MT 59722
406-846-2922
Innkeepers: Betty Stiehl and Ronda Stiehl

Nestled in the heart of gold country, and built in 1891, the mansion has over 6,500 square feet of living space on four levels with 2,000 square feet open to the public. Two fireplaces, with ornate carved oak and rosewood mantels, Tiffany style leaded stained glass pieces, oak hardwood floors and extensive ornate oak moulding have left a legacy of 19th century craftsmanship and style in this magnificent Queen Anne Victorian listed on the National Register of Historic Places. The five guest rooms are spacious and aspire to provide an intimate atmosphere, as well as warmth and comfort. The decor varies from charmingly nostalgic to eloquent. A full breakfast is served with entrees varying from day to day, and special arrangements available. Open year around. Conveniently located halfway between Glacier and Yellowstone National Parks, near many other points of interest.

Rates: $ - $$$$ Includes full breakfast. Children are welcome. Restricted smoking. We accept MasterCard, Visa and Am Ex.

ANGEL COOKIES

2 cups butter	1 cup cornstarch
1 cup confectioner's sugar	1 teaspoon almond extract
2 1/2 cups all purpose flour	1 1/2 cups finely chopped pecans

Preheat oven to 300°. Cream butter, add confectioner's sugar. Beat until light and fluffy. Combine flour and cornstarch. Add flour mixture and extract. Beat until well-blended. Add finely chopped pecans. Shape dough into 1" balls. Place on ungreased cookie sheets. Flatten with bottom of glass that has been dipped in flour. Bake about 20 minutes. Cookies will not brown. Let stand a few minutes before removing to wire rack to cool. Dust with confectioner's sugar. Makes approximately 8 dozen cookies.

CHICKEN DIANE

8 large boneless, skinless chicken breasts	4 heaping tablespoons dijon mustard
Water for cooking	1 bottle brandy extract
2 tablespoons chicken bouillon	1 cup fresh chopped parsley
3 cups water	3 bunches chopped green onion
1 cube unsalted butter	1 teaspoon lemon juice
2 tablespoons honey	

Cut chicken breasts into strips and place in large frying pan. Cook with water until done, for about 20 minutes, on medium heat. Remove chicken from pan, set aside. Place 3 cups water, bouillon, unsalted butter, honey, dijon mustard and brandy extract in pan and simmer for 10 - 15 minutes. Add chopped parsley, green onions and lemon juice. Simmer until vegetables turn color. Add cooked chicken and simmer until mixture starts to thicken. Serve over cooked angel hair pasta. Makes 8 servings.

Country Lane Bed & Breakfast

Route 2, Box 232 • Choteau, MT 59422
406-466-2816   406-466-2816 (FAX)
Web site: www.bbonline.com/mt/countrylane
E-mail: aarensmeyer@email.msn.com
Innkeeper: Ann Arensmeyer

This 5,000 square foot private home on the Spring Creek Game Preserve is located on 58 wooded acres, 1 1/2 miles north of Choteau. A peaceful country setting provides four spacious guest rooms with king and queen beds and an indoor solar-heated pool adjacent to the living room. A full country breakfast in the dining room affords gracious congeniality among guests. A gift shop features fine art, clay sculptures and mini quilts. Original art decorates the home and is created on the premises. Painting workshops are available on request with your hostess.

Rates: $ - $$$ Includes full breakfast. Children are welcome. No pets, please. Restricted smoking (outside only). We accept MasterCard and Visa.

Recipes From Country Lane Bed & Breakfast

BAKED EGGS IN TOMATO SHELLS

4 medium ripe tomatoes
Salt & pepper, to taste
1/2 teaspoon dried basil, crumbled
2 tablespoons melted butter

4 eggs
1/4 cup grated Swiss or Monterey Jack cheese
Fresh herbs for garnish

Cut a thin slice from top of each tomato. Scoop out pulp and seeds, discard. Turn tomatoes upside down to drain for ten minutes. Sprinkle inside of each with seasonings and spices. Butter each of four individual ramekins with melted butter. Place tomatoes in dishes, cut side up. Break an egg into each tomato shell. Bake at 350° for 30 - 40 minutes or until egg whites have set. Sprinkle with cheese and bake until melted, for about two minutes. Garnish with fresh parsley or other fresh herb. Makes 4 servings.

LUANNA'S BANANA BREAD

2 eggs, beaten
3 bananas, mashed
1 cup sugar
3 tablespoons sour cream or milk

3/4 cup oil
1 teaspoon baking soda
Dash of salt
1 3/4 cups flour

In medium bowl mix eggs and bananas. Add all remaining ingredients and mix gently. Bake in greased glass bread pan at 375° for 65 - 75 minutes. (Double recipe makes 7 mini foil loaves. Bake for 45 minutes) Makes 8 servings.

Creston Country Inn

70 Creston Road • Kalispell, MT 59901
406-755-7517
Web site: www.wtp.net/go/crestoninn
E-mail: creston.country.inn@worldnet.att.net
Innkeepers: Ginger Lockner and Rick Malloch

A charming 1920's farmhouse furnished with antiques provides guests with majestic mountain views and rural serenity. Located near Glacier National Park, the Bob Marshall Wilderness and the Jewel Basin, visitors experience some of Montana's most beautiful country at our doorstep. Just 9 miles to the east lies the art community of Big Fork, where the summer playhouse is a popular evening attraction. The *Inn* is located on 4.5 acres of pasture and gardens, and includes two big red barns with a panoramic view of the Northern Rockies and Flathead Valley. Guests can stroll the grounds along the creek, sit under the golden willows, or relax on the porch. There are four guest rooms, all with private baths. Each room boasts a special view of the mountains or valley and gardens.

Rates: $$$ Includes full breakfast. Children over age 8 are welcome. No pets or smoking, please. We accept MasterCard and Visa.

CRESTON EGG PUFF

8 eggs, room
  temperature
1/2 cup whole milk
1 cup grated cheddar
  cheese
1 1/2 cups chopped
  Canadian bacon

1/2 teaspoon dried basil
  (or 1 tablespoon fresh)
1/4 teaspoon white pepper
1/4 teaspoon salt
Crumbs of 1 English
  muffin (blended in
  blender)

Preheat oven to 350°. Spray 4 eight-ounce ramekins with non-stick spray. Whisk eggs and milk together. Add cheese, Canadian bacon and spices. Mix well. Whisk in English muffin crumbs. Bake for 30 - 35 minutes until puffed and golden. Garnish with basil sprig or chive blossom. Makes 4 servings.

EASY SOUR CREAM/CINNAMON COFFEE CAKE

<u>Cake Batter:</u>
1 box yellow cake mix
1 large box instant vanilla
  pudding mix
1 cup sour cream

1/2 cup milk
1/2 cup vegetable oil
  (scant)
4 beaten eggs

<u>Topping:</u>
1 cup sugar
1 tablespoon cinnamon

1 cup finely chopped
  pecans

Preheat oven to 350°. Mix batter ingredients together well in large bowl. Put half of batter in an oiled angel food cake pan. Pour half of topping mix over batter and swirl with a knife. Place remaining batter on top. Sprinkle with remaining topping and lightly swirl with knife. Bake for one hour or until toothpick inserted in center comes out clean. Makes 10 - 12 servings.

Deer Crossing Bed & Breakfast

396 Hayes Creek Road • Hamilton, MT 59840
406-363-2232   800-763-2232
Web site: www.wtp.net/go/deercrossing
E-mail: deercros@bitterroot.net
Innkeeper: Mary Lynch

Old West charm and hospitality at its best! Located along the Lewis and Clark Trail on twenty-five acres of tall pines and lush pasture overlooking the beautiful Bitterroot Valley. Start your day sipping a cup of fresh, hot coffee and watch the sun rise over the Sapphire Mountains. The sun room has become the favorite place to enjoy a hearty ranch breakfast featuring fresh fruit, homemade breads, egg casseroles ... Then plan your day to include hiking, horseback riding, fly fishing, exploring historical sites or relax on the deck and soak in the incredible views, the beauty and the quiet. Experience the Charlie Russell Suite, rich in western art and memorabilia, featuring a double jacuzzi tub; the Big Sky Suite with private balcony and ever changing views, two gracious guest rooms, or the Buck House, reminiscent of yesteryear. We invite you to "Kick off your boots, hang your hat and make yourself at home!"

Rates: $$$ Includes full breakfast. Children are welcome. Horses boarded. Restricted smoking, outside only. We accept MasterCard, Visa and Am Ex.

BAKED FRITTATA

3/4 cup diced green pepper
1 1/2 cups sliced mushrooms
1 1/2 cups chopped zucchini
3/4 cup chopped onion
1 clove garlic, minced
3 tablespoons olive oil

6 eggs, beaten
1/4 cup half and half
2 (8-ounce) pkgs. cream cheese, diced
1 1/2 cups cheddar cheese, shredded
2 cups bread, cubed
1 teaspoon salt
1/4 teaspoon pepper

Sauté green pepper (a little red pepper for color is nice), mushrooms, zucchini, onion and garlic in oil. Beat eggs with cream. Stir in cream cheese and cheddar cheese. Fold in bread, salt, pepper and sautéed vegetables. Pour into greased 9" x 13" casserole. Bake at 350° for one hour or until set in middle. Check with a knife that comes out clean. Cool 10 minutes before serving.

BROCCOLI QUICHE IN POTATO CRUST

2 medium potatoes, unpeeled & sliced
5 eggs
1 pkg. frozen, chopped broccoli
1 cup cheddar or Swiss cheese, shredded

1 cup cottage cheese
1/4 cup chopped onion
1 teaspoon dijon mustard
Salt, to taste
Dash of black pepper
Paprika, to taste

Slice unpeeled potatoes 1/4" thick. Arrange on bottom and sides of greased 9" pie pan. Thaw broccoli and squeeze dry. Beat eggs and add all other remaining ingredients. Pour into potato-lined pan. Dust with paprika. Bake at 375° for 45 minutes.

The Emily A. Bed & Breakfast

P.O. Box 350 • Seeley Lake, MT 59868
406-677-FISH
Web site: theemilya.com
E-mail: slk3340@montana.com
Innkeeper: Marilyn S. Peterson

Welcome home to a magnificent 11,000-square-foot log lodge. *The Emily A. Bed & Breakfast* overlooks a private lake with a waterfall on the Clearwater River, 5 miles north of Seeley Lake, Montana. Wake up rested to enjoy a fabulous breakfast served on grandmother's china, then explore our own 160 acres of scenic wilderness or the numerous winter and summer sports possibilities. Call for reservations and more information. We look forward to your visit. Remember your camera and binoculars!

Rates: $$$$ Includes full breakfast. Children and horses are welcome. We are smoke-free. We accept MasterCard, Visa and Travelers Checks.

EGGS BENEDICT

1 English muffin
Butter for muffin
1 slice ham, bacon or
  smoked salmon
May add spinach, thinly
  sliced onion, tomato
  or zucchini, if desired

2 eggs, poached
1/4 pound butter
3 egg yolks
1 tablespoon lemon
  juice
1 pinch cayenne
  pepper

Toast and butter English muffin. Layer meat, vegetables and poached eggs on top. Melt butter in heavy pan. Combine egg yolks, lemon juice and cayenne pepper in blender and mix. Remove blender cover and add melted butter very slowly. Mix for one minute or until thick. Pour sauce over muffin and serve immediately. Recipe can be doubled or tripled. Makes 1 serving.

SCANDINAVIAN FRUIT SOUP

1 papaya
1 mango
1 cup apple juice
1 cup non-fat milk

1 tablespoon honey
Lemon zest & cinnamon
  for garnish

Peel and seed fruit. Cut into squares. Puree in blender. Mix with apple juice, milk and honey. Decorate with lemon zest and cinnamon.

Fox Hollow Bed & Breakfast

545 Mary Road • Bozeman, MT 59718
406-582-8440   800-431-5010
Web site: www.bozeman-mt.com
E-mail: foxhollow@bozeman-mt.com
Innkeepers: Michael and Nancy Dawson

The wonder of Montana's Big Sky awaits you at *Fox Hollow Bed and Breakfast*. Located in the Gallatin Valley near the friendly town of Bozeman, *Fox Hollow* combines luxury accommodations with panoramic mountain views and wide open spaces. Travelers find a relaxed atmosphere surrounded by the peace of a country setting. Our five oversized guest rooms, each with a view of the Rockies, feature plush queen sized beds and private baths. You'll greet each morning with a delicious gourmet breakfast featuring such specialties as Eggs Benedict, baked omelets, homemade pastries and petite caramel rolls. In the evenings, settle down to a book or conversation in our comfortable living room, or join us by the fire in our family room. View the sunset, the stars or the shocking blue of the Big Sky from our wraparound deck, or indulge in a soothing soak in the hot tub. Come join Michael and Nancy and their friendly Montana hospitality.

Rates: $$$ - $$$$ Includes full breakfast. Children over age 12 are welcome. No pets, please. Restricted smoking. We accept MasterCard, Visa, Am Ex and Discover.

APPLE CINNAMON FRENCH TOAST

5 tablespoons butter
2 whole baking apples,
  peeled, cored & sliced
1 cup brown sugar,
  firmly packed
2 tablespoons corn syrup

1 teaspoon cinnamon
9 pieces French bread,
  sliced 1" thick
3 whole large eggs
1 cup milk
1 teaspoon vanilla extract

Day before: In skillet, melt butter at medium heat. Add apple slices and cook until tender. Add brown sugar, corn syrup and cinnamon. Cook, stirring, until brown sugar dissolves. Pour into 9" x 13" pan and spread evenly. Arrange bread in one layer on top of apples. Mix eggs, milk and vanilla. Pour over bread. Cover and refrigerate overnight. Bake at 375° for 30 - 35 minutes. Mixture should be firm and bread golden. Cool in pan for five minutes. Invert a tray over French toast and carefully turn both over to unmold so apple layer is on top. Spoon any remaining sauce and/or apples over French toast. Serve immediately topped with sweetened whipped cream. Makes 6 servings.

FRESH FRUIT WITH HONEY-LIME SAUCE

1 teaspoon finely
  shredded lime peel
4 teaspoons honey
1 tablespoon lime juice
1 (8-ounce) carton low-
  fat vanilla yogurt
1 whole banana, sliced
1 cup cantaloupe, cubed

1 cup honeydew melon,
  cubed
1 cup watermelon, cubed
2 whole kiwi fruits,
  peeled, halved length-
  wise, and sliced
1 bunch seedless grapes
  (red or green)

Shred lime peel into small bowl. Add honey and freshly squeezed lime juice. Stir until honey is dissolved. Stir in yogurt until well mixed. Mix fresh fruits among 8 champagne glasses; top with honey-lime sauce and serve immediately. Makes 8 servings.

BERRY COMPOTE MERINGUES

3 egg whites
1/4 teaspoon cream of tartar
1/8 teaspoon salt
1/2 cup sugar
1 teaspoon vanilla
1/2 cup finely chopped walnuts
1 cup frozen raspberries, thawed

1/2 banana
2 tablespoons strawberry all-fruit spread
1 1/2 tablespoons orange juice concentrate
1 cup fresh strawberries
1 cup fresh raspberries
1 cup fresh blueberries
2 ounces chocolate chips, melted

Preheat oven to 225°. Line cookie sheet with parchment paper. Draw six (3 1/2") circles on paper. Beat egg whites in large mixing bowl at medium until frothy; add cream of tartar and salt, continue beating until foamy. Beat in sugar 1 tablespoon at a time, gradually increasing mixer speed to high. Beat until stiff and glossy. Add vanilla and fold in nuts. Spoon or pipe meringue evenly into circles. With back of spoon, smooth shells and make a well in each. Bake for two hours. Turn off oven and let meringues cool in oven. Process frozen raspberries, banana, fruit spread and orange concentrate in blender until smooth. Strain through sieve into large bowl and stir in fresh berries. Refrigerate until serving time. To serve, arrange meringues on 6 dessert plates. Spoon Berry Compote into centers. Drizzle with melted chocolate and garnish with mint leaf. Makes 6 servings.

CHOCOLATE CHIP BARS

1/2 cup butter
3/4 cup brown sugar
1 whole egg
1 teaspoon vanilla
1 1/4 cups flour

1/2 teaspoon salt
1/2 teaspoon baking soda
3/4 cup chocolate chips
3/4 cup chopped walnuts

Cream butter and brown sugar. Add egg and vanilla and mix well. Add flour, salt and baking soda. Mix. Stir in chocolate chips and nuts. Grease 9" x 13" baking dish. Spread dough in baking dish and bake at 375° for 12 - 15 minutes. Cool and cut into bars. Makes 10 servings.

HERB CREAM SAUCED CHICKEN MANICOTTI

12 manicotti shells
16 ounces cream cheese
  with chives and onion
1 1/3 cups milk
1/2 cup grated Parmesan
  cheese
1 (10-ounce) pkg. frozen
  chopped broccoli,
  thawed and drained

2 cups diced, cooked
  chicken
1 (4-ounce) can mush-
  rooms, drained
1 (4-ounce) can pimentos,
  drained
1/4 teaspoon fresh ground
  black pepper
Paprika, to taste

Cook manicotti shells as package directs; rinse with cold water and drain. In saucepan melt cream cheese over medium heat until melted. Add milk and stir until smooth. Stir in cheese. Add 1 cup sauce to large mixing bowl. Stir in broccoli, chicken, mushrooms, pimentos and pepper for the manicotti filling. Cover the bottom of 9" x 13" x 2" baking dish with sauce. Carefully stuff each shell with about 1/3 cup filling and arrange in dish. Pour remaining sauce over shells. Sprinkle with paprika. Cover with foil and bake at 350° for 25 - 30 minutes or until heated. Makes 6 servings.

OVEN BAKED FIESTA OMELET

3/4 cup medium hot
  salsa
1 (14-ounce) can black
  beans, rinsed & drained
1/4 cup grated Parmesan
  cheese

2 1/2 cups cheddar
  cheese, grated
2 - 3 ounces chopped
  green chilies
6 whole large eggs
1 cup sour cream

Spray a 10" quiche pan with cooking spray. Cover the bottom with salsa. Top salsa evenly with black beans. Sprinkle Parmesan cheese evenly over beans. Top with cheddar cheese, then green chilies. Place eggs and sour cream in food processor and process until well blended. Pour slowly over chilies. Bake uncovered at 350° for one hour or until knife inserted in center comes out clean. Let omelet stand for 5 - 10 minutes before slicing. Slice into 6 pie-shaped wedges and serve with salsa and sour cream. Makes 6 servings.

NANCY'S FRESH FRUIT TOPPING

1 (8-ounce) pkg. straw-
berry flavored cream
cheese, softened

1 (7-ounce) jar
marshmallow cream

Beat all ingredients until creamy and serve with fresh fruit such as apples, pears, bananas, strawberries or kiwi. Makes 8 - 10 servings.

STRAWBERRY-KIWI MINI TARTS

Crust:
1 cup flour
1/2 cup confectioner's
sugar
1/2 cup butter

Cream Filling:
1 (4-ounce) pkg. cream
cheese
1/4 cup sugar
1/8 teaspoon fresh lemon
juice

Topping:
1/2 pint fresh straw-
berries, stemmed &
mashed
2 tablespoons sugar
1/2 tablespoon cornstarch

Garnish:
1 whole kiwi fruit,
peeled & sliced
1/2 pint fresh straw-
berries, washed,
drained & sliced

For crust, combine flour and sugar; cut in butter until mixture clings together. Pat into 24 mini-muffin cups, using about 2 teaspoons of dough for each cup. Shape dough about halfway up sides, forming mini-tarts. Bake at 325° for 10 - 15 minutes or until golden brown. Watch closely as they brown very quickly. For filling, combine cream cheese, sugar and lemon juice. Beat until smooth and spread over cooled pastry. Refrigerate pastries. For topping, cook mashed strawberries over medium heat until juice is bright red. Strain juice to remove pulp. Add sugar and cornstarch to juice and cook until thickened. Cool. Spread juice over cream cheese mixture. Chill tarts for 1 - 2 hours before serving. Garnish with kiwi and sliced strawberries and serve.

BLACK & WHITE COOKIES

2 1/2 cups flour
1/2 teaspoon salt
1 cup unsalted butter
3/4 cup sugar
1 whole large egg, at
  room temperature
1 teaspoon vanilla

2 teaspoons fresh, grated
orange zest
1 (4-ounce) pkg.
Hershey's semi-sweet
chocolate chips, melted
1 (4-ounce) block white
chocolate, melted

In medium bowl stir together flour and salt. In large bowl beat softened butter with mixer for 30 seconds until creamy. Beat in sugar until well combined. Beat in egg, vanilla and orange zest well. On low speed gradually beat in flour mixture just until combined. Place dough into pastry bag fitted with plain #4 or #5 tip. Pipe batter onto baking sheets in 2 1/2-inch strips and about 1" apart. Bake at 350° for 11 - 13 minutes. Cool cookies on sheet on wire rack for about one minute. Transfer to rack and cool completely. Melt chocolates. Fill two separate pastry bags fitted with 1/8" tips with semi-sweet and white chocolates. Pipe random lines of semi-sweet chocolate over cookies. Repeat with white chocolate. Store in air-tight container at room temperature up to 5 days. Makes about 4 1/2 dozen cookies.

OVEN-PUFFED PANCAKE

1/2 cup flour
2 tablespoons sugar
1/4 teaspoon salt
1/2 cup milk
2 whole eggs
2 tablespoons butter

1/2 cup sugar
1 tablespoon cornstarch
1/2 cup orange juice
2 tablespoons orange
  liqueur or orange juice
3 cups fruit, sliced

Lightly spoon flour into measuring cup and level off. In medium bowl combine first five ingredients. Beat with wire whisk or beaters until smooth. Place 2 tablespoons butter in 9" pie plate and melt in oven just until sizzling (2 - 4 minutes). Remove pan and tilt to coat bottom with butter. Immediately pour batter into hot pan and bake at 425° for 14 - 18 minutes until golden brown. For sauce, combine 1/2 cup sugar and cornstarch in small saucepan. Stir in orange juice and liqueur. Stir and cook over medium heat until mixture thickens (about 7 minutes). Remove pancake from oven and split in half. Arrange sliced fruit (strawberries, blueberries, blackberries, raspberries, kiwi, banana, peaches, etc.) on top, dust with powdered sugar and drizzle with orange sauce. Makes 2 servings.

Foxglove Cottage Bed & Breakfast

2331 Gilbert Avenue • Missoula, MT 59802
406-543-2927 (FAX) 406-543-5324
Innkeepers: John Keegan and Tony Cesare

Foxglove Cottage is a cozy 100-year-old house surrounded by a lovely three-tiered garden situated in the Rattlesnake Valley just minutes from downtown Missoula, the University of Montana and the Rattlesnake Wilderness Area. The house is furnished with antiques and decorated with fresh and dried flowers from the Victorian cottage garden. Each of the three charming guest rooms has a TV and VCR (there is an extensive video library). Sun Room. Airport Pickup. Complimentary drinks. "A Romantic Get-away ~ in Town!"

Rates: $$$ Includes continental plus breakfast. No pets or smoking, please.

ARTICHOKE SALAD

4 whole artichokes
Water for cooking
3 (6-ounce) jars artichoke hearts (not drained)
5 green onions, diced
1 jar capers, drained
2 tablespoons Dijon mustard

2 tablespoons white wine vinegar
2 tablespoons olive oil
2 tablespoons chopped parsley
8 slices red pepper for garnish

Cook the artichokes in a large covered kettle in 1" of water for one hour (or until done). Drain and cool. Cut out the heart, dice and put in large bowl, but save the leaves. Add the remainder of ingredients (except red pepper) to the bowl and marinate for at least one hour. When ready to serve, arrange the leaves in a circle on each individual salad plate. Heap the heart marinade in the center and dribble juice in the leaves. Garnish with red pepper slices. Makes 8 servings.

LEEK AND POTATO SOUP "BONNE FEMME"

4 leeks, sliced
3 large potatoes, peeled & diced
4 cups chicken broth
4 cups water
1/2 teaspoon white pepper
1/2 teaspoon salt

2 small zucchini, sliced in razor-thin rounds
10 small mushrooms, sliced in razor-thin slices
Chopped chives for garnish

Trim the leeks and slice. Wash thoroughly and drain in colander. Peel and dice the potatoes. Put chicken broth and water in large kettle, add leeks, potatoes, white pepper and salt. Cook at a slow boil for one hour or until potatoes are very done. Let cool. Puree in a blender and return to kettle. (This may take several steps.) Just before serving, bring back to a boil. Add zucchini and mushrooms and cook for 5 minutes. Garnish with chopped chives. Makes 8 - 10 servings.

Gracenote Gardens Bed & Breakfast

1558 South 6th Street West • Missoula, MT 59801
406-543-3480
Innkeepers: Bob and Billie Gray

Gracenote Gardens B&B, located in the center of the city is just minutes away from all shopping, university and cultural events, while being only 1/2 hour to 1 hour away from wilderness hiking, fishing and camping. Featuring two large second-floor rooms decorated with floral motifs. The Sonata Room overlooks the pool and waterfall. (Private bath, $90 dbl. - $80 sing.) The Duet features twin beds and private bath. ($70 dbl. - $60 sing.) Accommodation tax not included. We love gardening, music, books, eating, visiting and delight in having friends share it all with us.

Rates: $$ - $$$ Includes full/continental plus breakfast. Children over age 6 are welcome. No pets, please. Restricted smoking (outdoors only).

GRACENOTE GARDEN PANCAKES

2 cups Krusteze
  pancake mix
1/2 cup oat bran
2 tablespoons wheat
  germ

2 cups buttermilk
2 eggs (or equivalent in
  egg substitute)
1/2 cup molasses
2 tablespoons cooking oil

Heat griddle while preparing batter. Mix dry ingredients. Add buttermilk, eggs, molasses and oil. Beat until well blended. (Batter may have some small lumps.) Add water one tablespoon at a time if desired, for thinner batter. Pour onto hot, lightly oiled griddle. Turn when batter bubbles and bottom is nicely browned. Serve with warmed syrup or warm applesauce and whipped cream. Makes 12 - 4" pancakes.

LYRICAL GRAPEFRUIT

1/2 grapefruit, sectioned
1 - 2 tablespoons brown
  sugar

Chopped nuts, if desired
Maraschino cherry and
  mint leaves for garnish

Section grapefruit, sprinkle with brown sugar and nuts, if desired. Place under broiler and broil until edges are browned and sugar is melted and bubbling. (Use only a metal pan under broiler.) Remove to serving dish and garnish with cherry and/or mint leaves as desired. Makes 1 serving.

HIDDEN M●●SE LODGE
Whitefish, Montana

Hidden Moose Lodge

1735 East Lakeshore Drive • Whitefish, MT 59937
406-862-6516   888-SEE-MOOSE (reservations)
Web site: www.wtp.net/go/hiddenmoose
E-mail: seemoose@digisys.net
Innkeepers: Kent and Kim Taylor

We feature three whirlpool suites and five beautifully decorated lodge rooms. Located 1 1/2 miles from downtown Whitefish, 5 miles from the Big Mountain Ski and Summer Resort, and just 30 minutes from the west entrance to Glacier National Park. All rooms have balconies, private entries, private baths and king or queen-sized log beds, cable TV, VCR's and telephones. The great room features a floor to ceiling river rock fireplace, framed by large picture windows overlooking a forest complete with deer trails. The back deck features a waterfall, an outdoor fireplace and, hidden in the trees off the main deck, is a built-in hot tub. Hearty "no need for lunch" breakfasts are served in the dining room. Entrees include Huckleberry Buttermilk Pancakes, Chorizo Quiche or Eggs À La Hidden Moose with fresh fruit, juice and a selection of teas and coffee. Your innkeepers are avid skiers, river rafters and enthusiastic fly fishermen, willing to share with you all the great places in western Montana.

Rates: $$$ - $$$$ Includes full breakfast. Children are welcome. No pets, please. Restricted smoking. We accept MasterCard, Visa and Discover.

❖ *Recipes From Hidden Moose Lodge* ❖

CHORIZO QUICHE

1 (24-ounce) pkg. frozen shredded hashbrowns, thawed
1/3 cup melted butter
1 pound chorizo sausage, fried and drained
1 cup shredded hot pepper cheese (we like Tillimook)

1 cup shredded sharp cheddar cheese
1/4 cup green chilies
1/2 cup half and half
3 - 4 eggs
Salt and pepper, to taste

Press thawed hashbrowns into greased pie plate or baking dish. Brush crust with melted butter and bake at 425° for 20 - 25 minutes until golden. Remove from oven and sprinkle with cooked sausage, cheeses and chilies. Beat half and half, eggs, salt and pepper. Pour over cheese and sausage. Bake uncovered at 350° for 30 - 40 minutes or until knife comes out clean. We serve salsa (Hot Chile Mama's) and sour cream on the side.

EGGS À LA HIDDEN MOOSE

8 slices extra wide bacon, cooked, but not crisp

8 eggs
Toasted English muffins
Cayenne pepper, to taste

Hollandaise Sauce:
1/2 cup butter
1 1/2 tablespoons lemon juice

3 egg yolks
4 tablespoons boiling water

Spray muffin pan with cooking spray. Line pans with individual slices of bacon. Break an egg into each cup. Bake at 350° until yolks are done, but just runny. For Hollandaise Sauce, melt butter slowly and keep warm. Barely heat lemon juice. Have boiling water ready with a tablespoon measure. Place egg yolks in top of a double boiler. Beat with wire whisk until they begin to thicken and add 1 tablespoon boiling water. Beat again until eggs begin to thicken. Repeat this process until you have added 3 more tablespoons of boiling water. Beat in warm lemon juice. Remove from double boiler and beat sauce well with whisk. Slowly add melted butter. Remove eggs from pan with rubber spatula. Place on toasted English muffin and top egg with a tablespoon of sauce and a sprinkle of cayenne pepper. Serve with hashbrowns and fruit. Yummy!

Johnstad's B&B and Log Guest House

03 Paradise Lane - P.O. Box 981 • Emigrant, MT 59027
406-333-9003
Web site: www.wtp.net/go/johnstad
E-mail: rjohnstad@aol.com
Innkeepers: Ron and Mary Ellen Johnstad

Our Bed & Breakfast offers three spacious guest rooms all with private baths and spectacular views of the Absoraka Mountain Range and the Yellowstone River Valley. Each room is uniquely decorated to create a warm atmosphere for our guests. Our breakfasts are hearty, spiced with lively conversation. We feature pancakes made with a family recipe, and there is always a supply of freshly baked homemade cookies for our guests in the gathering room. Available also is our fully furnished Log Guest House with kitchen, dining area, living room, three bedrooms, two baths and laundry facilities for a private getaway. We have lived in Montana for twenty years and raised our family here. Our knowledge about the area provides an excellent base for any Montana vacation. Ask Ron, an avid fly fisherman, how to tie a fly. We are just thirty-six miles north of Yellowstone Park.

Rates: $$$ - $$$$ Includes full breakfast. Children are welcome in Guest House. No pets or smoking, please. We accept MasterCard, Visa and Discover.

GRANDMOTHER'S GINGER COOKIES

1 cup shortening	1/2 teaspoon ground
1 cup sugar	cinnamon
1 beaten egg	1/2 teaspoon ground
2 tablespoons molasses	cloves
2 cups flour	1/2 teaspoon ground
1/4 teaspoon salt	nutmeg
1 1/2 teaspoons baking	1/2 teaspoon ground
soda	ginger

Cream shortening and sugar. Add egg and molasses. Add remaining ingredients that have been sifted together. Roll into balls and dip into sugar. Place on greased cookie sheet. Bake at 350° for 10 - 12 minutes. Makes approximately 36 cookies.

SWEDISH PANCAKES

2 eggs, separated	1/2 teaspoon baking
2 tablespoons sugar	soda
1/2 cup cream	1/2 cup flour
3/4 cup buttermilk	1/4 teaspoon salt

Beat egg yolks; add sugar, cream, buttermilk and baking soda. Beat well. Add flour and salt and beat until very smooth. Fold in egg whites. Bake on hot griddle or in Plett pan. Serve with butter and hot syrup. Or to be authentically Swedish - serve with lingonberries and slightly whipped cream. Makes 2 servings.

The Josephine Bed & Breakfast

514 North 29th Street • Billings, MT 59101
406-248-5898
Web site: www.thejosephine.com
E-mail: josephine@imt.net
Innkeepers: Doug and Becky Taylor

The Josephine Bed & Breakfast offers an oasis of quiet seclusion within walking distance of downtown Billings' shopping, museums restaurants and entertainment. Throughout the *Inn*, antiques, old photographs and unique tablescapes provide a pleasing, comfortable atmosphere for guests. Relax and unwind in *The Josephine's* parlor, complete with cable TV and VCR, an upright piano and cozy seating, or sink into a comfy chair in our study filled with books, board games and a writing desk with phone and dataport. We offer complimentary snacks and beverages. The newspaper, health club guest passes, menus from area restaurants and information about local attractions are provided for your convenience. Five individually decorated guest rooms, each with telephone with dataport and its own private bath. Two are suites with sitting rooms that can accommodate up to four people. After a restful night, indulge yourself with freshly ground coffee or tea and a delicious gourmet breakfast served in our sunny dining room.

Rates: $$ - $$$ Includes full breakfast. Children over age 6 are welcome. No pets or smoking, please. We accept MasterCard, Visa, Am Ex and Discover.

EGG AND CHEESE STRATA

4 slices of bread, toasted
& crusts trimmed
4 ounces grated cheddar
cheese
4 eggs
2 cups milk

1/2 teaspoon dry mustard
1/8 teaspoon onion
powder
Dash of pepper
Cubed ham or bacon bits,
optional

Toast bread and trim off crusts. Cut into 1/2" cubes. Put the equivalent of one slice of bread in each of four individual serving, ungreased, round-bottomed ramekins. (Grease if bottom is flat.) Top bread with grated cheese. In small bowl mix milk, eggs, dry mustard and onion powder until smooth (do not whip). Sprinkle pepper on top. Pour egg mixture into individual ramekins. Cover and refrigerate overnight. In the morning uncover and bake at 325° for one hour. Makes 4 servings.

RANCH QUICHE LORRAINE

1 - 8" baked and cooled
pie shell
1 cup grated Swiss cheese
3 large eggs
1 1/4 cups heavy
whipping cream

1 pkg. ranch dressing
mix (about 2
tablespoons dry mix)
2 tablespoons bacon
bits, optional

Preheat oven to 400°. Sprinkle cheese in cooked pie shell. Whisk eggs until frothy. Add other ingredients to egg mixture and mix. Pour over cheese. Bake at 400° for 15 minutes. Reduce heat to 350° and bake for 15 - 20 more minutes until center is set. Final baking may take up to 30 minutes. Cool. Makes 8 servings.

The Keith House

The Keith House, A Bed & Breakfast Inn

538 Fifth Avenue East • Kalispell, MT 59901
800-972-7913
Web site: www.keithhousebb.com
E-mail: keithbb@digisys.net
Innkeepers: Don and Rebecca Bauder

Located on a quiet tree-lined street in the heart of Kalispell's Historic
District, *The Keith House* is one of the largest and finest homes built
in Montana during the early years of the 20th century. Listed on the
National Register of Historic Places, it has been meticulously
restored, furnished with comfortable antiques, vintage linens, lovely
English china and silver. Each of six guest rooms has a private bath,
cozy chairs and lofty down comforter on a luxurious bed. Spacious
common rooms invite conversation with other guests, and a secluded
library with comfortable, over-stuffed chairs offers quiet reading in
front of one of the home's beautiful fireplaces. A hearty breakfast is
served each morning in the dining room from a magnificent Belgian
antique sideboard. A large wraparound veranda with wicker chairs
allows you to put your feet up with a glass of wine or lemonade at the
end of an adventurous day in the Flathead Valley.

*Rates: $$$$ Includes full breakfast. Older children are welcome.
No pets or smoking, please. We accept MasterCard,
Visa and Am Ex.*

PECAN FRENCH TOAST

1 cup margarine, melted	8 eggs, beaten
1 cup brown sugar, packed	1 1/2 cups milk
1 cup pecans, chopped	1 loaf French bread, cut into 1 1/2" thick slices

In 12" x 15" jelly roll pan, melt margarine as oven preheats at 350°. Stir in brown sugar and sprinkle with pecans. In separate bowl beat eggs and stir in milk. Dip slices of bread into egg mixture and arrange over brown sugar and pecan mixture in pan. Pour any remaining egg mixture over bread. Bake for 35 - 40 minutes. Invert each slice onto serving plate. Makes 6 - 8 servings.

STRAWBERRY SHORTCAKE MUFFINS

2 cups flour	1 cup heavy whipping cream
1 teaspoon baking powder	1 teaspoon vanilla
3/4 cup sugar	1 cup diced fresh straw-berries, well-drained
1/2 cup butter	
1 egg	

In medium bowl mix flour, baking powder and sugar. Cut in butter with pastry cutter. In separate bowl mix egg, whipping cream and vanilla. Add egg mixture all at once to flour mixture and mix well with wooden spoon. Gently fold in strawberries. Spoon batter into 12 greased muffin tins. Bake in preheated oven at 350° for 25 minutes. Remove and cool completely. They are very rich and will fall apart if not cooled. Dust with powdered sugar if desired, and serve with strawberry butter. Makes 12 muffins.

Lehrkind Mansion Bed & Breakfast

719 North Wallace Avenue • Bozeman, MT 59715
406-585-6932 800-992-6932
Web site: www.bozemanbedandbreakfast.com
E-mail: lehrkindmansion@imt.net
Innkeepers: Jon Gerster and Christopher Nixon

Listed in the National Register, built in 1897, the *Lehrkind Mansion* offers one of Montana's finest Queen Anne Victorian Mansions. A spacious yard and gardens, porches and a three-story tower are among the mansion's spectacular features. Period antiques fill every nook. The music parlor features Victrolas, a large piano and a rare century-old seven-foot tall music box! Queen-sized high-back oak beds, plush comforters and overstuffed chairs provide relaxation, and a large therapeutic hot tub will soak away aches of an active day. Just seven blocks from Bozeman's historic Main Street shopping district, the mansion is also only 1 1/2 hours from Yellowstone. Hosts Jon and Christopher served as park rangers in Yellowstone and can give detailed advice on area attractions. Christopher's gourmet breakfasts are fresh from scratch! A stay at the *Lehrkind Mansion* is not just a room for the night - it's an experience!

Rates: $$ - $$$$ Includes full breakfast. Children are welcome. No pets or smoking, please. We accept MasterCard, Visa and Am Ex.

DARK CHERRY POPPY SEED MUFFINS

2 cups all purpose flour
3 teaspoons baking powder
1/2 teaspoon salt
1/2 cup sugar
2 tablespoons poppy seed
1 cup buttermilk

1/3 cup canola oil (scant)
1 egg
1 teaspoon almond extract
1 cup chopped fresh or frozen dark sweet cherries
Additional poppy seed

Streusel Topping:
1/4 cup whole wheat or all purpose flour
2 tablespoons brown sugar

1/4 teaspoon ground cinnamon
2 tablespoons slightly softened butter

Heat oven to 400°. Spray medium muffin cups with cooking spray. Prepare Streusel Topping by cutting butter into other three ingredients and reserve. Sift flour, baking powder, salt and sugar into large bowl. Add 2 tablespoons poppy seed and mix in thoroughly. In separate bowl beat buttermilk, oil, egg and almond extract. Add to flour mixture and fold in until flour is moistened. Fold in chopped cherries. Divide batter among muffin cups to about 3/4 full. Sprinkle with Streusel Topping and additional poppy seed. Bake for 22 - 24 minutes or until golden brown. Allow to cool in muffin tins for 30 seconds and remove. Makes 12 muffins.

SPINACH PORTABELLA ROULADE

1 1/2 cups portabella mushrooms, chopped (about 3/4 of a large 1)
1 teaspoon oil
1/2 cup all purpose flour
1 cup milk
4 large or 5 medium eggs
1/2 teaspoon salt

2 tablespoons butter, melted
1/4 - 1/3 cup chopped red onion
1 1/2 cups shredded Swiss cheese
1 1/2 cups finely chopped fresh spinach, divided

Heat oven to 400°. Line 15 1/2" x 10 1/2" x 1" jelly roll pan with aluminum foil. Generously spray foil with cooking spray. Sauté chopped portabella mushrooms in oil and set aside. Beat next five ingredients until well blended and pour into pan. Sprinkle with onion and mushrooms. Bake until eggs are set, approximately 12 minutes. Immediately sprinkle with cheese and 1 cup spinach. Roll up, beginning at narrow end, using foil to lift and roll omelet, using a wide spatula to separate and roll. Cut across roll into about 6 slices (approximately 1 1/2" wide). Serve in center of plate surrounded with 1/2 cup spinach for garnish. Serve immediately. Makes 6 servings.

Montana Mountain Lodge

1780 Highway 89 North • White Sulphur Springs, MT 59645
406-547-3773
E-mail: mtlodge@ttc-cmc.net
Innkeepers: Jean Cooney Roberts and Dan Funston

The *Montana Mountain Lodge* is a unique lodging experience. It's secluded. It's peaceful. A perfect respite for the traveler who wants to enjoy authentic western hospitality. Your hostess has a family history in the state dating back to 1863. Conveniently located between Glacier and Yellowstone National Parks on scenic Highway 89, 22 miles north of White Sulphur Spring. This is the real Montana, wide valleys, high prairie and pine covered mountains. See the land, changed little from when the first settlers came searching for gold or land to make a new life. *The Lodge* with fine mountain views has a steaming guest jacuzzi, wood burning stoves and five comfortable rooms each with private bath. Open year-around we offer hiking, fishing, bird watching, great wildlife, skiing (downhill and cross-country) and snowmobiling. Delightful evening meals are offered to our guests. Arrangements need to be made in advance. Reservations recommended.

Rates: $$ Includes full breakfast. Children are welcome. No pets, please. Restricted smoking.

Recipes From Montana Mountain Lodge

CRANBERRY BARLEY PUDDING BREAKFAST

2 quarts water
1 cup pearl barley,
  rinsed and drained
4 cinnamon sticks
3 cups water

3/4 cup sugar
1 1/2 cups raisins
2 cups cranberries
2 tablespoons lemon
  juice

Bring 2 quarts water to a boil; add barley and cinnamon sticks; simmer slowly, uncovered, until water is absorbed, for about 45 minutes. Stir occasionally. Add remaining ingredients and continue simmering slowly until most of the liquid is absorbed, for approximately 30 minutes or longer. Serve warm or cold with brown sugar, milk or cream or whipping cream. Makes 8 - 12 servings.

GRANDMA'S COOKIES

3 1/2 cups flour
1 - 1 1/2 teaspoons
  baking soda
1/2 teaspoon salt
1 1/2 teaspoons nutmeg

1 1/2 cups sugar
1 cup butter
3 eggs
2 teaspoons vanilla
1 cup buttermilk

Combine all dry ingredients; set aside. Combine remaining ingredients, mixing well. Add flour mixture to other ingredients to form a soft dough. Knead slightly until dough does not stick. Roll dough out to 1/4" thickness, cut with a 2" round cookie cutter or drinking glass. Place on cookie sheet and bake at 350° for 10 minutes. Makes 3 dozen cookies.

Osprey Inn Bed & Breakfast

5557 Highway 93 South • Somers, MT 59932
406-857-2042
Web site: www.ospreybnb.com
E-mail: ospreyin@cyberport.net
Innkeepers: Wayne and Sharon Finney

On the shore of Flathead Lake relax and unwind in a warm, hospitable and cozy atmosphere, plus also participate in all sorts of summer vacation pastimes nearby. Choose from four rooms with a view and private baths; enjoy a full breakfast. We are conveniently located so that most of the activities and attractions in this area are only a short drive away. Activities range from hiking, horseback riding, golfing and sailing to birding and photography. Glacier National Park is only 44 miles away. Excellent restaurants are nearby and one of the finest, the Montana Grill, is within walking distance. The scenery is always magnificent and, of course, changes with the seasons. Relax on the deck or around the evening campfire. Canoe to the islands or swim off the dock. Kick back at sunset in the hot tub after a day of touring.

Rates: $$$$ Includes full breakfast. Inn is not appropriate for children. No pets, please. Restricted smoking. We accept MasterCard and Visa.

BANANAS' JJ

4 bananas	1 teaspoon rum extract
1 tablespoon butter	Whipped cream
1 tablespoon brown sugar	Ground nutmeg

Slice peeled bananas lengthwise. Sauté sliced bananas in butter, brown sugar and rum extract for five minutes, turning occasionally. Serve in ramekins with whipped cream and just a small sprinkle of nutmeg on top.

BOGGENBARB CRISP

Filling:

3 quarts diced rhubarb	1 cup white sugar
1 cup dried or fresh cranberries	1/4 cup cornstarch
1/2 cup brown sugar	1 teaspoon cinnamon
	1/2 cup orange juice

Topping:

1/2 pound butter, softened	1 cup brown sugar
3 cups rolled oats	1 teaspoon allspice

Mix all filling ingredients in a large bowl, then pour into a 9" x 13" pan. In separate bowl combine softened butter with oats, brown sugar and allspice. Mix well. Combine topping ingredients and place over top of filling. Bake at 350° for one hour or until liquid from filling bubbles up through the topping. Serve with whipped cream or vanilla ice cream. Makes 8 servings.

Outlook Inn Bed & Breakfast

P.O. Box 177 - 175 Boon Road • Somers, MT 59932
406-857-2060   888-857-VIEW
Web site: www.webby.com/montana/outlook
E-mail: outlook@digisys.net
Innkeepers: Michelle McGovern and Todd Ahern

Nestled above the Westshore of Flathead Lake in Somers, Montana ...
our spacious, yet cozy, lodge-like home sits on seven private acres
and offers all of the amenities. Curl up in front of the river rock
fireplace and watch the colors of the sky change and reflect on the
lake. Enjoy osprey or bald eagles as they soar above the *Inn.* Relax
in your own private, jetted tub or double shower. Sun yourself on the
huge log deck overlooking the lake and Rocky Mountains. Walk to
the lake, boat rentals, great restaurants and more. In the winter,
energize yourself with a gourmet breakfast, then choose between two
downhill ski resorts or x-country ski, snowshoe or snowmobile. All
four of our guest rooms feature queen size beds, private baths and a
deck with spectacular lake and mountain views. And children are
always welcome. We have two of our own!

*Rates: $$ (off-season) - $$$ (high-season) Includes full or
continental breakfast. Children are welcome. No pets, please.
Restricted smoking (outside only). We accept MasterCard, Visa,
Am Ex and Discover.*

FLATHEAD LAKE MONSTER POTATOES

2 pounds frozen
  hashbrown potatoes
1 can cream of mushroom
  soup
2 cups grated cheddar
  cheese
2 cups sour cream

1/2 cup chopped onion
1/2 cube of butter, melted
1 cup cooked elk sausage
Topping:
2 cups crushed Corn
  Flakes cereal
1/4 cup butter, melted

Combine hashbrowns, soup, cheese, sour cream, onion, 1/2 cube of melted butter and elk meat. (Can use summer sausage instead.) Turn into greased 9" x 13" pan. Stir topping ingredients together. Sprinkle over potato mixture. Bake at 350° for 30 minutes. (May add 1/2 cup green or red bell pepper for added zest.) Makes 8 side dishes.

FRESCANTS

1 dozen eggs
Grated orange peel from
  half an orange
Juice from half an orange

1 tablespoon vanilla
1/4 cup milk
1 dozen croissants,
  cut in half

Mix eggs, orange peel, orange juice, vanilla and milk in shallow pan or dish. Cut croissants in half. Dip each half in batter. Place on heated non-stick griddle. Cook until lightly browned, then flip. Serve with huckleberry syrup and butter. Makes 8 servings.

Paradise Gateway B&B and Guest Cabins

P.O. Box 84 • Emigrant, MT 59027
406-333-4063   800-541-4113
Web site: www.wtp.net/go/paradise
E-mail: paradise@gomontana.com
Innkeepers: Pete and Carol Reed

If you've dreamed about a romantic hideaway amid the natural glories of America's Big Sky Country, next to Yellowstone National Park, *Paradise Gateway B&B and Guest Log Cabins* is just the place for you. As you eat your hearty gourmet breakfast in this spacious country home on the banks of the Yellowstone River - within view of the breathtaking 10,900 foot tall Emigrant Peak - you'll feel like you're in paradise, indeed. Guests have the luxury of choosing rooms in the Inn or quaint modern log cabins with 100 acres to roam. All with private baths, decorated in French country. A 'cowboy' treat tray is served to guests after they have enjoyed a memorable horseback ride or fishing with a top-quality guide in the nation's premier trout waters - the Yellowstone River, which is *Paradise Gateway's* front yard. Guests return frequently as they know they can find the promise of another exciting tomorrow.

Rates: $$$$ Includes full breakfast. Children are welcome. No pets, please. Smoke-free Inn and Cabins - outdoor smoking only. We accept MasterCard and Visa.

LEMON CURD

3/4 cup sugar
1/2 cup margarine
1/3 cup lemon juice

Grated rind of 2
lemons
3 eggs, beaten

Place all ingredients in top of double boiler over hot water. Stir until well blended and thick, about 5 minutes. Stores well in refrigerator. Serve over bread pudding or with scones. Makes 8 - 10 servings.

PARADISE GATEWAY SCONES

2 cups white flour
3 tablespoons white sugar
3 1/2 teaspoons baking
  powder
1/4 teaspoon salt
2/3 cup margarine

1/3 cup dried cherries,
  blueberries, dates,
  raisins or cranberries
3/4 cup milk
Additional milk
  for tops

Sift together flour, sugar, baking powder and salt. Cut in margarine with pastry cutter or fingers until mixture resembles coarse oatmeal. Add fruit and mix together. Add 3/4 cup milk. Mix lightly with a fork until just blended. Add 1 or 2 additional tablespoons of milk if necessary to hold mixture together. Preheat oven to 425°. Divide dough into two equal parts and turn on floured board. Pat into circles 1" in thickness. Handle only enough to pat into shape. Score with a knife halfway through to form four portions in each circle. Brush with 1 tablespoon milk. Bake for 18 - 20 minutes. Makes 8 scones.

COLD OVEN GLAZED POUND CAKE

2 sticks margarine
1/2 cup Crisco
3 cups sugar
5 eggs
3 cups white flour
1 teaspoon baking powder

1 cup milk
1 teaspoon vanilla
1 teaspoon orange
  flavoring
1 teaspoon lemon
  flavoring

Lemon Glaze:
1 1/2 cups confectioner's
  sugar

3 tablespoons lemon
  juice

Cream margarine, Crisco and sugar thoroughly, add eggs one at a time and beat well. Sift together flour and baking powder, add alternately with milk. Add flavorings and bake in greased tube pan at 325° for one hour and 15 minutes to one hour and 30 minutes. Start with cold oven (do not preheat). When done, cool for 10 minutes and invert pan on rack. Mix glaze ingredients and pour over warm cake. Makes 12 - 16 servings.

TOMATO QUICHE

2 cups Bisquick mix
1/2 cup milk
6 medium tomatoes,
  sliced
1 1/2 bunches green
  onions, chopped
1 teaspoon salt

1 teaspoon pepper
2 tablespoons sweet basil
1 tablespoon dill weed
1 cup mayonnaise
2 cups shredded cheese
  (may use half feta and
  half cheddar)

Mix together Bisquick and milk and press into 10" pie pan. Slice tomatoes over crust. Mix green onions, salt, pepper, basil and dill and sprinkle over tomatoes. Mix mayonnaise and cheese; spread over top. Bake at 350° for 40 - 45 minutes. Great for vegetarians!

SPINACH PHYLLO

2 red onions, finely
chopped
1/2 pound mushrooms,
sliced
1 tablespoon butter
1 (3-ounce) pkg. cream
cheese
1 (10-ounce) pkg.
spinach, thawed &
squeezed dry
1/2 teaspoon salt
Freshly ground black
pepper, to taste

Juice of 1/2 lemon
2 tablespoons all purpose
flour
1 large egg, slightly
beaten
1/2 cup sour cream
1/2 pound phyllo pastry,
thawed
1/2 cup unsalted butter,
melted
1 pound Swiss cheese,
thinly sliced (or feta
cheese)

In large saucepan briefly sauté onions and mushrooms in 1 tablespoon butter. Stir in cream cheese and cook until melted. Add next five ingredients. Blend and heat thoroughly. In small bowl mix egg and sour cream; stir into hot spinach mixture; set aside. When working with phyllo dough, keep it covered with a damp cloth whenever possible. Unroll phyllo dough and lay flat on cutting surface. Place 7" x 12" baking dish on stack of phyllo, cut around edges of pan with a sharp knife. Discard trimmings. Using a pastry brush, brush 6 sheets phyllo with melted butter and layer them in greased baking pan. Spoon half of the spinach mixture over phyllo, spreading evenly to within 1" of pan edges. Cover with thin slices of Swiss cheese. Repeat layers of buttered phyllo, spinach and cheese. Brush 4 phyllo sheets with melted butter and place on top. Score top sheets with sharp knife to define serving pieces. Bake uncovered at 375° for 35 minutes or until top is golden brown.

WALLA WALLA VIDALIA ONION BAKE

1 large Vidalia onion
1 tablespoon brown
sugar
1 teaspoon butter

1 tablespoon bread
crumbs
1 - 2 ounces blue cheese
Freshly ground pepper

Cross-cut peeled onion and flex open like a flower. Open the petals and add remaining ingredients in order. Wrap in foil. Bake at 325° for about 45 minutes or until tender. Makes 1 - 2 servings.

Querencia

P.O. Box 184 - Highway 89 South • Emigrant, MT 59027
406-333-4500   888-603-4500
Web site: www.querencia.com
E-mail: joe@querencia.com
Innkeepers: Joe and Linda Skaggs

Elegantly rustic and warmly hospitable, *Querencia* has five guest rooms with queen or twin beds and private entrances from spacious decks, each with magnificent views of the Absaroka and Crazy Mountains. Three tiled bathrooms with showers are private or semi-private and a family suite with two bedrooms, bath, sitting area and private deck is available. *Querencia* features radiant floor heat with individual thermostats and Douglas fir floors throughout, making this mountain retreat very comfortable. The gathering area features an antique wood stove and stone hearth, the perfect interior to share the day's adventures and plan tomorrow's. The library holds a sampling of Montana's best literature and folklore as well as an extensive video collection. A riverside grill and picnic area is available to guests. Children are welcome to camp out under the stars close to the comfort of *Querencia*. The Inn can accommodate corporate retreat or family reunion.

Rates: $$$ - $$$$ Includes continental plus breakfast. Children are welcome. We accept pets. Restricted smoking. We accept MasterCard, Visa and Am Ex.

Recipes From Querencia

CRANBERRY ORANGE BREAD

2 cups flour
1 teaspoon salt
1 teaspoon baking soda
1 teaspoon baking powder
1/2 cup vegetable
  shortening (at room
  temperature)
1 1/4 cups sugar

2 large eggs, lightly
  beaten
1/2 cup buttermilk
1/2 teaspoon vanilla
1 tablespoon grated
  orange rind
1 cup fresh whole
  cranberries

Glaze:
1/8 cup orange juice   1/4 cup powdered sugar

Preheat oven to 350°. Combine dry ingredients in large bowl. In another bowl thoroughly mix shortening, sugar, eggs, buttermilk, vanilla and orange rind. Add flour mixture; mix well. Fold in cranberries gently. Grease two 5" x 9" x 3" bread pans. Pour in batter. Bake for 40 minutes; test with toothpick. When toothpick comes out clean, bread is done. Make glaze by mixing orange juice and sugar; let set until sugar dissolves. Leave bread in pan, drizzle with glaze. Remove carefully from pans; let rest on cooling rack for 30 minutes before slicing. Better if served next day.

TART BERRY MUFFINS

1 1/2 cups all purpose
  flour
1 teaspoon baking powder
1/4 teaspoon salt
6 tablespoons unsalted
  butter
1 cup sugar

2 large eggs
3 teaspoons grated lemon
  peel
1/2 cup milk
1 1/2 cups fresh rasp-
  berries, or frozen, but
  thawed & drained

Preheat oven to 325°. Butter muffin tin. Combine flour, baking powder and salt in small bowl. Using electric mixer, cream butter with sugar in large bowl until light and fluffy. Add eggs one at a time, beating well after each addition. Add lemon peel. Mix in dry ingredients alternately with milk. Fold in raspberries. Spoon batter into prepared muffin pan. Bake until golden brown and toothpick inserted into center comes out clean, about 20 - 25 minutes. Makes 18 muffins.

The Sanders - Helena's Bed & Breakfast

328 North Ewing • Helena, MT 59601
406-442-3309
Web site: www.sandersbb.com
E-mail: thefolks@sandersbb.com
Innkeepers: Rock Ringling and Bobbi Uecker

Nationally acclaimed as one of the 100 best bed and breakfasts in the United States and Canada, *The Sanders* offers elegant accommodations steeped in the history of Montana's capital city. Built in 1875 by Harriet and Wilbur Sanders and restored 112 years later, this historical register home combines the spirit of days gone by with the comforts of today. Seven guest rooms are graced with original furnishings and reflect grand turn-of-the-century living. Each richly detailed room has its own in-room bath, TV, phone and dataport as well as a charming view of Helena and the surrounding valley and mountains. A full breakfast is served each morning in the wainscotted dining room; refreshments await arriving guests each afternoon. Located in the heart of Helena, *The Sanders* is within three blocks of St. Helena's Cathedral, the Original Governor's Mansion, and historic Last Chance Gulch. Also nearby are the State Capitol, the Montana Historical Museum, and fine restaurants and shops.

Rates: $$$ - $$$$ Includes full breakfast. Children are welcome. No pets or smoking, please. We accept MasterCard, Visa, Am Ex, Discover and Diners.

FRENCH TOAST WITH SAUTÉED FRUIT

3 tablespoons butter
1 cup sliced strawberries
1 cup sliced apple
1 cup sliced orange
1 cup raspberry jam
4 tablespoons triple sec
 liqueur
1 teaspoon nutmeg

4 eggs
1 cup milk
2 tablespoons sugar
Juice of 1 orange
Juice of 1 lime
1 1/2 teaspoons vanilla
8 slices French bread,
 sliced 1/2" thick

Preparing the fruit: Melt butter in shallow pan over medium heat and sauté the prepared fruit. Add jam, triple sec and nutmeg. Reduce heat and occasionally stir fruit very gently until hot. For toast: Combine eggs, milk, sugar, juices and vanilla in large bowl and mix thoroughly. Dip bread slices into egg mixture, coating both sides thoroughly. Cook on griddle or in skillet over medium heat until both sides are brown, turning just once. Place French Toast on serving plates and glaze with 1/2 - 3/4 cup of sautéed fruit. Sprinkle with powdered sugar. Makes 8 servings.

JAKE'S FAVORITE CRANBERRY MUFFINS

1/4 cup sugar
1 1/4 cups flour
2 teaspoons baking
 powder
1/4 teaspoon salt
1 egg, beaten
1 tablespoon vegetable oil

1/4 cup milk
1/2 cup fresh orange
 juice
Grated rind of 1 orange
1 cup fresh cranberries,
 chopped
1/4 cup chopped walnuts

Preheat oven to 400°. Grease muffin tin. Combine first four ingredients in large bowl. In another bowl, combine egg, oil, milk, orange juice and rind. Add this mixture to the dry ingredients, stirring just until blended. Fold in cranberries and walnuts. Fill muffin tins 3/4 full and bake for 15 minutes or until done. Makes 12 muffins.

JOE'S BREAKFAST SHAKE

1 banana	1 teaspoon vanilla
1 cup raspberries	1/2 cup orange juice
1 cup vanilla-flavored yogurt	8 ice cubes (about 1 cup) Mint garnish (opt.)

In the order listed above place all ingredients except mint in the blender. Blend thoroughly. Serves 2 in stem goblets with mint garnish.

THE SANDERS' B&B CHOCOLATE ZUCCHINI COOKIES

1/2 cup milk	4 tablespoons cocoa
1 teaspoon lemon juice or 1 teaspoon vinegar	1/2 teaspoon baking powder
1/2 cup margarine, softened	1 teaspoon baking soda
1/2 cup vegetable oil	1/2 teaspoon cinnamon
1 3/4 cups sugar	1/2 teaspoon cloves
2 eggs	2 cups finely diced zucchini
1/2 teaspoon vanilla	1 (12 ounce) pkg. semi-sweet chocolate chips
4 cups flour	

To the milk, add lemon juice or vinegar and allow to stand for five minutes, to "sour" it. Cream margarine, oil and sugar. Add eggs and vanilla and combine thoroughly. Beat sour milk into margarine mixture. Mix flour, cocoa, baking powder, soda, cinnamon and cloves in separate bowl until well combined. Add this to creamed mixture and beat very well. Fold in zucchini and chocolate chips. Using a teaspoon, drop dough onto a greased cookie sheet and bake at 350° for about 12 minutes. Cookies have a cake-like texture and do not spread too much. Makes approximately 12 dozen small cookies.

THE SANDERS' B&B TENTH ANNIVERSARY PORRIDGE

1/3 cup Wheat Montana 7-grain cereal	1 tablespoon raisins or currants
1 cup water	Pinch of ground ginger
1/2 apple, chopped	6 - 7 coarsely chopped almonds
1/4 teaspoon cinnamon	

Combine all ingredients in a saucepan and bring to a gentle simmer over low heat, stirring occasionally. The longer and slower the cooking the creamier the porridge, so let your preference be your guide. Remove from heat and cover, allowing it to sit for several minutes before serving. Brown sugar, maple syrup or honey are favorite toppings. Makes 1 serving.

THE SANDERS' HOLIDAY FRENCH TOAST

1 (8-ounce) pkg. cream cheese, at room temperature	1/3 cup walnuts
	10 slices of bread
1/4 cup apricot jam	4 eggs
4 ounces mixed dried fruit	1 cup milk
	2 teaspoons vanilla
	1 tablespoon sugar

Whip cream cheese until soft. Add jam. Chop dried fruit and walnuts and blend them into cream cheese mixture. Spread this mixture on five slices of bread and cover each with a second slice to make a sandwich. Combine eggs, milk, vanilla and sugar in large bowl. Dip each sandwich into egg mixture and cook on buttered griddle or skillet, turning once so that all are nicely browned and the filling softens. Serve with warm maple syrup. Makes 5 servings.

Swan Hill Bed & Breakfast

460 Kings Point Road • Polson, MT 59860
406-883-5292 800-537-9489
Web site: www.wtp.net/go/swanhill
Innkeepers: Lawrence and Sharon Whitten

Welcome to our spacious redwood home which is modern in amenities and has the warmth of western hospitality. Awaken to gourmet breakfasts in our formal dining room or under an umbrella table on the deck where you can bask in the morning sun and the deer will join you. For your enjoyment we have an indoor pool surrounded by outdoor decks to view Flathead Lake and the Mission Mountains. To accommodate you we have three queen bedrooms and one twin bedroom. The fifth room is a suite with bedroom, living room, jacuzzi bath and private patio. Conference facilities are also available. We are handicapped accessible. Three pet cats are in residence. Check-in time 4 - 7 P.M. Check-out time 11 A.M.

Rates: $$$ - $$$$ Includes full breakfast. Children over age 16 are welcome. Pets are allowed. Restricted smoking. We accept MasterCard and Visa.

FRENCH CREAM FOR FRUIT

1 cup whipping cream,
  whipped
1/3 cup powdered sugar
1/2 cup sour cream

1/2 teaspoon grated
  lemon rind
2 ounces triple sec
  liqueur

Whip cream. Fold in other ingredients. Refrigerate. Serve over fruit cup. Makes 8 servings.

HAPPINESS BLENDER HOLLANDAISE

1/2 cup butter
6 egg yolks
4 tablespoons lemon juice

1 teaspoon salt
Dash of tabasco sauce

Melt butter to bubbling in saucepan. In blender blend yolks, lemon juice, salt and tabasco sauce for one minute. Add bubbling butter slowly to blender from the top. Blend for two minutes. Great served over Eggs Benedict. Makes 1 1/2 cups of sauce.

The Timbers Bed & Breakfast

1184 Timberlane Road • Ronan, MT 59864
406-676-4373   800-775-4373
Web site: www.bbhost.com/thetimbers
E-mail: timbers@ronan.net
Innkeepers: Doris and Leonard McCravey

This stunning inn has a spectacular view of the Mission Mountains, and faces into a glacier that has snow in it year round. It is secluded on 21 acres and borders the Mission Wilderness area. Built in 1990, the house is a blend of modern comfort and old, country charm. The spacious common room has a large fireplace and is glassed in to provide a spectacular view of the Mountains. Cathedral ceilings, hand-hewn beams and barn-wood dining area give the inn a sophisticated yet warm country feel. There is one two-room suite with private bath that sleeps 2 - 5 people. It is perfect for a romantic honeymoon, or even a family holiday. Relax on the wraparound deck and enjoy the abundance of wildlife, or listen to Leonard's wonderful stories of his 27 years on the Pro-Rodeo circuit. Come share our valley with us and experience the best of the old and the new West.

Rates: $$ - $$$$ Includes full breakfast. Children are welcome. No pets, please. Restricted smoking. We accept MasterCard and Visa.

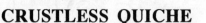

CRUSTLESS QUICHE

1 1/4 cups milk
1/2 cup biscuit mix
3 tablespoons butter
3 eggs
Dash of salt & pepper
Dash of garlic powder
(opt.)

Dash of cayenne pepper
1 cup diced ham, bacon
or shrimp
2 green onions, chopped
4 ounces sliced
mushrooms
1 cup grated sharp cheese

Preheat oven to 350°. Combine the first seven ingredients in food processor and mix well. Turn into greased, deep 9" or 10" pie plate. Mix together meat, onions, mushrooms and cheese. Sprinkle over egg mixture, poking the meat mixture down into the egg mixture with a knife. Bake until the top is golden, for about 45 minutes. Let stand for 10 minutes before serving. Makes 8 servings.

PECAN JAM SQUARES

1/2 cup butter or
margarine, cut into
chunks
1/2 cup brown sugar

1 cup flour
1/2 cup strawberry jam
or jam of choice

Topping:
1 cup pecans
2 eggs
1 cup brown
sugar
1 teaspoon vanilla

1 tablespoon flour
1/4 teaspoon baking
powder
3 tablespoons powdered
sugar for garnish

For crust: In food processor process butter or margarine, brown sugar and flour for 20 seconds. Press into 8" square pan or 9" x 13" pan. Bake at 350° for 15 minutes. Spread with jam. For topping: Chop nuts coarsely (8 - 10 seconds). Empty bowl. Process remaining ingredients except powdered sugar until mixed (10 - 15 seconds). Add pecans and mix in with 2 or 3 quick on/off turns. Spread over crust. Bake for 25 minutes longer. Cool completely and sprinkle with powdered sugar. Makes 8 - 12 bars or 24 bars.

TIME After TIME Bed & Breakfast

197 Pistol Lane • Victor, MT 59875
406-642-3258
Web site: www.montana.com//timeaftertime
E-mail: timeaftertime@montana.com
Innkeeper: Trish Hatfield

TIME After TIME B&B invites you to experience the beautiful
Bitterroot Valley. Spend your leisure time amid spectacular scenery
and a million acres of wilderness. Tourist friendly communities offer
hiking, hunting, fishing, golfing and biking. Centrally located just 40
minutes from Missoula, the Bitterroot Valley is noted for its fine crafts
people and unique products. Come for the Microbrewery Festival or
County Fair, just 8 miles south in Hamilton. You may wish to enjoy
the peace and quiet on the 10 acres of secluded park-like grounds.
Walk through our woods on picturesque pathways. Birds, deer and
wildflowers may be seen among the pines, cottonwoods and aspens.
Practice fly-casting on our own small pond or fish the Bitterroot
River. *TIME After TIME* offers three spacious and comfortable bed-
sitting rooms with private and shared baths. We serve a sumptuous
full gourmet breakfast and light refreshments from 4 - 5:30 P.M.

Rates: $$ Includes full breakfast. Children over age 3 are welcome.
No pets, please. Restricted smoking.

CRUSTLESS VEGGIE QUICHE

2 medium zucchini,
  thinly sliced
1 small onion, sliced
  thinly into rings
1 small jar marinated
  artichokes
2 cups grated jack or
  cheddar cheese

5 large eggs
1/2 cup cream or milk
1 teaspoon salt
1/4 teaspoon pepper
1 teaspoon basil or
  dill spice

Lay zucchini slices on bottom of quiche pan, pie plate or 6" x 9" casserole. Spread onion rings on top. Cut artichoke hearts into smaller wedges. Place cheese over all, be sure to cover to edges. Use wire whisk to beat eggs, cream and spices together. Pour evenly over the top of the cheese. Bake at 375° for 30 - 45 minutes until browned and puffy. Makes 6 servings.

SPICY CHICKEN CASSEROLE

6 boneless, skinless
  chicken breasts or
  tenderloins, cut into
  1" - 2" cubes
1/2 cup chopped onion
2 tablespoons butter
1 can cream of
  mushroom soup

1 cup sour cream
1/4 cup white wine or
  sauterne
1 (6 - 8 ounce) can
  chopped green chilies
3 cups cooked rice
1 cup grated sharp
  cheddar cheese

Sauté chicken cubes with onion in the butter. Set aside. Mix together soup, sour cream and wine. Heat just until steaming. Add chicken, onions, chilies, cooked rice and 1/2 cup cheese. Mix well. Pour into casserole dish. Cover with remaining cheese. Bake at 350° for 30 - 40 minutes until brown and bubbling. Makes 6 - 8 servings.

Trout Springs Bed & Breakfast

721 Desta Street • Hamilton, MT 59840
406-375-0911   888-67TROUT
Web site: www.wtp.net/go/troutsprings
E-mail: tsprings@bitterroot.net
Innkeepers: Maynard and Brenda Gueldenhaar

Nestled against the backwaters of the Bitterroot River in the Heart of
the Bitterroot Valley lies an elegant and spacious B&B. The location
is a haven for beaver, birds and deer with trout ponds and beautiful
gardens. A true paradise for nature lovers and sportsmen alike. Our
guests are welcome to fish for trout in our ponds, fish the waters of
the Bitterroot or enjoy the serenity of nature by listening to the
whispers of the river. There are six bedrooms, all have king size beds
and private baths. Enjoy fireplaces, TV, laundry, spacious decks, an
evening campfire, old-fashioned popcorn popper and ice cream
maker. Have fun singing around the 1926 player piano. The house
features original western art designed and built by the proprietors in
their own gallery on the premises. Four-course breakfast with fresh
trout and fresh homemade breads. AAA 3-diamond rated. Selected
for "Bed & Breakfasts" by Frommers.

Rates: $$$ Includes full breakfast. Children over age 12 are
welcome. No smoking, please. We accept MasterCard, Visa,
Am Ex and Discover.

SCRAMBLED EGGS & SMOKED TROUT IN A MUSHROOM SAUCE

1/4 cup butter or margarine
6 large eggs, lightly beaten
2/3 cup half and half
Salt, to taste
1/2 cup sliced mushrooms (or 4-ounce can)
1/4 cup flour
1 1/2 cups milk
3/4 cup smoked trout
Pepper, to taste

Heat oven to 350°. Place 1 tablespoon butter in skillet; combine eggs, half and half and salt. Cook over medium-low heat. The eggs should be moist, do not overcook. Spray 9" x 12" baking dish with cooking oil. Put scrambled eggs in bottom and up sides of dish. Place 1 tablespoon butter in skillet over medium-high heat. Add about three-quarters of the mushrooms and cook until lightly browned, about 3 minutes. To the skillet add 3 tablespoons butter and sprinkle with the flour. Gradually stir in milk and cook, stirring constantly, until mixture is smooth and thickened, about 10 minutes. Add three-quarters of smoked trout, simmer for 5 minutes and add pepper, to taste. Pour skillet mixture over scrambled eggs. Top with remaining mushrooms and smoked trout. Bake uncovered until heated through, about 15 minutes. Garnish with parsley or chives. Makes 4 servings.

TROUT SPRINGS ALMOND CASHEW GRANOLA

1/2 cup canola oil
1/2 cup honey
1/2 teaspoon salt
1 tablespoon vanilla
1/2 cup sesame seeds
1 cup wheat germ
2 cups unsweetened coconut
1/2 cup cashews
1/2 cup sliced almonds
7 cups large flake oatmeal

In large saucepan heat oil, honey, salt and vanilla until mixture is blended. Turn heat off and stir in remaining ingredients. Make sure each ingredient is coated with honey mixture. Heat oven to 350°. Put cereal in large pan. Bake for 15 minutes. Once it has begun to brown stir it every 5 - 10 minutes. I cook mine for about 45 minutes. Remove from oven and cool before pouring into storage jars. Most of the ingredients can be found in health food stores.

Whitefish River Inn

51 Penney Lane • Columbia Falls, MT 59912
406-257-6052 888-622-6052
Web site: www.whitefishinn.com
E-mail: aliyoung@ptinet.net
Innkeeper: Alison Young

Overlooking the Whitefish River and bordered by fields and woods, the large contemporary farmhouse is surrounded by gardens, green lawns and spacious decks. The *Inn's* three rooms each have a private bath, lush duvets, soft robes and views to the natural surroundings. The dramatic Montana river rock fireplace, soaring ceiling and indigenous woods welcome you. Relax on the deck, watching a beaver ripple the river and an osprey glide to a high branch. Curl up in the window seat of the cozy den with a book or a movie. Soak in the hot tub under the stars, listening to coyotes yipping at the moon. Enjoy a hearty breakfast buffet and sip locally roasted coffee in the sun room or on the deck, while white tail deer nibble alfalfa and hummingbirds shimmer in the morning light. Explore the *Inn's* nature trails and swimming hole or the Flathead Valley and Glacier National Park.

Rates: $$$$ Includes full breakfast. Children over age 10 are welcome. No pets or smoking please. We accept MasterCard and Visa.

COLD CURRY AND RICE SALAD

2 chicken breasts, cooked & diced, if desired
2 small boxes Rice-A-Roni or Uncle Ben's chicken rice mix
2 chopped green onions
1/2 green pepper, diced

2 (6-ounce) jars marinated artichoke hearts, diced
1 small can sliced black olives
1/3 cup mayonnaise
1/4 teaspoon curry

Cook chicken and dice. Cook rice mix according to package directions without adding butter. Add green onions and peppers. Drain artichokes, saving marinade. Add artichokes and olives to rice mixture. Simmer until onions and peppers are tender. Add chicken. Combine marinade, mayonnaise and curry. Whip until smooth. Add to rice mixture. Chill before serving. Makes 8 - 10 servings.

SALMON SPREAD

1 1/2 cups smoked salmon
1 (8-ounce) pkg. cream cheese, softened
1 clove garlic, finely minced

3 tablespoons minced green onion
1/4 teaspoon salt
2 tablespoons Worcestershire sauce
1 tablespoon lemon juice

Mix all ingredients together. Serve on crackers, squares of toast or toasted English muffins cut into fourths. Makes 2 1/2 cups of spread. Other smoked fish may be used in place of salmon.

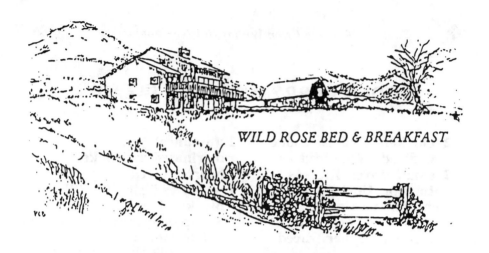

WILD ROSE BED & BREAKFAST

Wild Rose Bed & Breakfast

1285 Upper Tom Burke Road • Gallatin Gateway, MT 59730
877-763-4692 (toll-free)
Web site: www.avicom.net/wildrose
E-mail: gallatin@avicom.net
Innkeepers: Dennis and Diana Bauer

The Wild Rose Bed & Breakfast is a comfy, country home located in the beautiful Gallatin Valley. Nestled against a hill, it faces the spectacular snow-covered Spanish Peaks Mountains. Buffalo can be seen grazing across the valley. Deer and elk forage on the hillside. Three delightful guest rooms are named after nearby blue ribbon streams, the Madison, Jefferson and Gallatin, which join to form the Missouri at a point along the route of the Lewis & Clark Expedition. A full breakfast is served in the sunny dining room. A fireplace provides a cozy atmosphere after an exhilarating day of adventure. Popular activities include sight-seeing in Yellowstone National Park, visiting museums and novelty shops in Bozeman, skiing at nearby Big Sky and Bridger Bowl Resorts, cross-country skiing, snowshoeing, kayaking, rafting, fishing, hiking and horseback riding. Dine gourmet or on meals with a western flair in nearby restaurants.

Rates: $$ - $$$ Includes full breakfast. Children are welcome. No pets or smoking, please. We accept MasterCard and Visa.

BLUEBERRY BAKED FRENCH TOAST

4 slices Texas toast (1"
  sliced white bread)
2 1/2 cups milk
6 eggs
1 teaspoon cinnamon or
  mace

1/4 cup flour
2 tablespoons brown
  sugar
2 tablespoons - 1/4 cup
  butter
1 cup blueberries

Butter a 9" square baking pan. Overlap bread slices to fill pan. Combine milk and eggs. Pour over bread slices, cover and refrigerate overnight. Next day, remove from refrigerator 3/4 hour before baking and preheat oven to 375°. In small bowl combine cinnamon or mace, flour, brown sugar and butter. Spread over bread. Cover bread with blueberries. Bake 45 - 60 minutes or until done. Makes 6 - 8 servings.

GARDEN FRITTATA

4 slices bacon, browned
1 medium chopped onion
1 1/2 cups lightly steamed
  vegetables (asparagus,
  broccoli, zucchini, etc.)
2 - 4 tablespoons parsley

1 tablespoon fresh basil
  (or 3/4 teaspoon dried)
6 beaten eggs
1/4 cup Parmesan cheese
1 1/2 cups grated Swiss
  cheese

In 11" skillet brown bacon, crumble and set aside, removing most of the drippings. In remaining drippings, sauté onion. Add crumbled bacon, steamed vegetables, herbs, eggs and Parmesan cheese. Top with Swiss cheese. Place a lid on skillet and allow to cook on low heat until nearly set. Finish under broiler in oven until top is brown. Makes 6 servings.

MONTANA TRAVEL GUIDE

In Montana, travel is a journey of time and space. It is an end in itself. In the chiseled faces of rock walls, it is a glimpse of eternity. In pristine waters that reflect vast, clear skies, it is cause for hope. In mile-upon-mile of natural landscapes, it is tonic for the world-weary traveler. Montana invites you to leave that world behind and rediscover your soul in Big Sky Country.

In a land shaped by space and sky, the views are forever. Uncluttered by society's diversions, Montana is a place to reconnect with the earth and its many gifts. Forests and badlands, river valleys and deserts, alpine meadows and grassy prairies are all part of the view in Montana. From the eastern plains to the skytop peaks and mile-high valleys of the Rocky Mountains, Montana sets a stage of sweeping proportions.

Montana's parks and protected lands range from the heavenly peaks of Glacier National Park to the fiery caldrons of Yellowstone. In between are national forests and battlefields, historic ranches, canyons, wildlife preserves and a state park system that protects the best of Montana: ghost towns, badlands, buffalo jumps and a range of quality recreational opportunities. Montana has been described as one giant park. But it's not true. Montana's landscape and history are too varied to be confined to just one!

Montanans are in good company with the wildlife that actually outnumber them. Montana supports the largest grizzly bear population south of Canada, the largest migratory elk herd in the nation, the largest breeding population of trumpeter swans in the lower 48 and the nation's largest native herd of Rocky Mountain bighorn sheep - all in all, a magnificent array of wildlife whose very survival depends on unspoiled habitat. With patience and a pair of binoculars, people can view these and many other species in the wild.

In Montana, the West is more than a label or a trend. It is a way of life that is rooted in history and hopeful about the future. It defines Montana both as a place and as a people. The West doesn't put on airs. Its simple truth appears in the weathered faces of people who work the land, the abandoned homesteads of early dreamers, the native costumes of Indian dancers and the easy smile of most everyone you'll meet.

Montana is a young state whose history lives quietly at buffalo jumps and historic battlefields, in pictograph caves, weathered ghost towns, humble missions and magnificent turn-of-the-century mansions. It springs to life at summer festivals like the Montana Cowboy Poetry Gathering and Custer's Last Stand Re-enactment. It goes underground in Havre, and surfaces in Butte. It flows through Montana along the Missouri River, original highway of the West.

Adventure travel in Montana is the journey made personal. Somehow, it is not enough merely to see Big Sky Country. This land of peaks and canyons, whitewater gorges and meandering streams, powder snow and sunshine begs to be experienced. Montana is the perfect place to fulfill your passion. Whether it is floating or fly fishing, biking, hiking or skiing, it can and should be done in Montana!

Montanans find common ground at festivals that celebrate their shared history as well as their diversity. Take in the Miles City Bucking Horse Sale, the Crow Fair Powwow, the Flathead Balloon Festival or Scobey's Pioneer Days, and you, too, will catch the spirit of celebration. Summer is high season for fairs and rodeos, Indian powwows, sporting events, music and ethnic festivals, but the fun doesn't end when the temperature falls and school starts. Crowds are down and the weather can be surprisingly mild in the off-season. Bozeman's Winter Fair, St. Patrick's Day in Butte, the C.M. Russell Art Auction in Great Falls and Missoula's International Wildlife Film Festival make it clear that celebrations are never out of season in Montana!

Montana invites exploration. For every federally designated scenic backroad and byway, there are countless unofficial ones. Much of the newly developed "Trail of the Great Bear" lies in Montana. An international scenic corridor that links Yellowstone National Park with Canada's Banff National Park, this trail celebrates the history, culture and natural resources of some of the last wild country on the continent.

It has been nearly 200 years since two of America's most heralded frontiersmen traveled more than 8,000 miles on what is now the Lewis and Clark Trail to unlock the West for an ambitious, young nation. Well over a quarter of their journey was spent in Montana, and much of what they saw here remains unchanged. Remote stretches of the Missouri and Yellowstone Rivers and physical landmarks, including Capt. Clark's signature, remain for explorers today.

Moviemaking and Montana go hand in hand. Directors like Robert Redford (*A River Runs Through It*) and Ron Howard (*Far and Away*) chose from 147,138 square miles of dramatic backdrops and numerous authentic, Old West sites. Some favorite locations for movies, commercials, television and "stills" have been the stately Moss Mansion in Billings, the revived neighboring ghost towns of Virginia City and Nevada City, incomparable Glacier National Park, aptly named Paradise Valley, golden wheat fields near Great Falls and the history-rich territorial prison in Deer Lodge. If you're in the area, you might enjoy visiting a location where one of your favorite movies was filmed to experience Montana's star quality first-hand.

Montana travel information provided by:
TRAVEL MONTANA
800-VISIT MT
Web Site: http://travel.mt.gov

Montana Bed and Breakfast Association

"Being the Best in the Last Best Place" is the motto of the Montana Bed and Breakfast Association. This motto is one each of our members takes to heart. Welcome to Big Sky country, a place of flowing streams and crisp fresh air. An abundance of wonderful hiking and biking trails, fishing, golfing, skiing, sightseeing and genuine hospitality is found in Montana. What better way to explore and experience these wonders, than in an Association approved Bed and Breakfast? From an historic mansion in the city to a luxurious log home in the mountains, MTBBA offers the discerning traveler a wide range of top-of-the-line quality inns. MTBBA inns are professionally inspected and approved on a consistent basis for the highest degree of comfort, cleanliness, hospitality and safety. Association members can be confident in referring their guests to another MTBBA member inn. Our members are truly proud of Montana and what it has to offer. We cordially invite you to experience this splendor from the comfort and convenience of an MTBBA approved property.

Please visit the Montana Bed and Breakfast Association Internet web site at www.mtbba.com or contact us at 1-800-453-8870 for a free Directory of Members.

NOTES

NOTES

NOTES

NOTES

NOTES

ORDER FORM

To order by phone, please call 800-457-3230.
Visa and MasterCard accepted.

Indicate the quantity of the book(s) that you wish to order below.
Please feel free to copy this form for your order.

MAIL THIS ORDER TO:

Winters Publishing
P.O. Box 501
Greensburg, IN   47240

Quantity

Quantity	Title	Price	Total
_____	*Heart Healthy Hospitality*	$10.95 each	_____
_____	*Mountain Mornings*	$10.95 each	_____
_____	*American Mornings*	$12.95 each	_____
_____	*What's Cooking Inn Arizona*	$12.95 each	_____
_____	*Pure Gold - Colorado Treasures*	$9.95 each	_____
_____	*Colorado Columbine Delicacies*	$10.95 each	_____
_____	*Inn-describably Delicious - Illinois*	$9.95 each	_____
_____	*Indiana B&B Assn. Cookbook*	$9.95 each	_____
_____	*Hoosier Hospitality - Indiana*	$10.95 each	_____
_____	*Savor the Inns of Kansas*	$9.95 each	_____
_____	*Sunrise in Kentucky*	$9.95 each	_____
_____	*Another Sunrise in Kentucky*	$9.95 each	_____
_____	*Just Inn Time for Breakfast - Michigan*	$10.95 each	_____
_____	*Be Our Guest - Missouri*	$9.95 each	_____
_____	*A Taste Of Montana*	$10.95 each	_____
_____	*Palmetto Hospitality - South Carolina*	$10.00 each	_____
_____	*South Dakota Sunrise*	$10.95 each	_____
_____	*A Taste of Tennessee*	$9.95 each	_____
_____	*A Taste of Washington State*	$14.95 each	_____
_____	*Good Morning West Virginia!*	$12.95 each	_____

Shipping Charge $2.00 1st book, $1.00 each additional.   _____

5% Sales Tax (IN residents ONLY)   _____

TOTAL   _____

Send to:

Name: _____

Address: _____

City: _____ State: _____ Zip: _____

Phone: (____) _____

Bed & Breakfast Cookbooks from Individual Inns

Heart Healthy Hospitality - Low Fat Breakfast Recipes / The Manor At Taylor's Store
Features 130 low-fat breakfast recipes. Special lay-flat binding. 160 pgs. $10.95

Mountain Mornings - Breakfasts and other recipes from The Inn at 410 B&B
Features 90 tempting recipes. Special lay-flat binding. 128 pgs. $10.95

National Bed & Breakfast Cookbook

American Mornings - Favorite Breakfast Recipes From Bed & Breakfast Inns
Features breakfast recipes from 302 inns throughout the country, with complete information about each inn. 320 pgs. $12.95

State Bed & Breakfast Association Cookbooks

What's Cooking Inn Arizona - A Recipe Guidebook of the AZ Assn. of B&B Inns
Features 126 recipes from 21 Arizona inns. 96 pgs. $12.95

Pure Gold - Colorado Treasures / Recipes From B&B Innkeepers of Colorado
Features over 100 recipes from 54 Colorado inns. 96 pgs. $9.95

Colorado Columbine Delicacies - Recipes From B&B Innkeepers of Colorado
Features 115 recipes from 43 Colorado inns. Special lay-flat binding. 112 pgs. $10.95

Inn-describably Delicious - Recipes From The Illinois B&B Assn. Innkeepers
Features recipes from 82 Illinois inns. 112 pgs. $9.95

The Indiana Bed & Breakfast Association Cookbook and Directory
Features recipes from 75 Indiana inns. 96 pgs. $9.95

Hoosier Hospitality - Favorite Recipes from Indiana's Finest B & B Inns
Features over 125 recipes from 54 Indiana inns.   128 pgs. $10.95

Savor the Inns of Kansas - Recipes From Kansas Bed & Breakfasts
Features recipes from 51 Kansas inns. 112 pgs. $9.95

Sunrise in Kentucky
Features 100 recipes from 51 Kentucky inns. 112 pgs. $9.95

Another Sunrise in Kentucky
Features 110 recipes from 47 Kentucky inns. 112 pgs. $9.95

Just Inn Time for Breakfast (Michigan Lake To Lake B&B Association)
Features recipes from 93 Michigan inns. Special lay-flat binding. 128 pgs. $10.95

Be Our Guest - Cooking with Missouri's Innkeepers
Features recipes from 43 Missouri inns. 96 pgs. $9.95

A Taste Of Montana - A Collection of Our Best Recipes
Features 84 recipes from 33 Montana inns. 96 pgs. $10.95

Palmetto Hospitality - Inn Style (South Carolina)
Features over 90 recipes from 47 South Carolina inns. 112 pgs. $10.00

South Dakota Sunrise - A Collection of Breakfast Recipes
Features 94 recipes from 37 South Dakota inns. 96 pgs. $10.95

A Taste of Tennessee - Recipes From Tennessee Bed & Breakfast Inns
Features 80 recipes from 40 Tennessee inns. 96 pgs. $9.95

A Taste of Washington State
Features 250 recipes from 83 Washington inns. 192 pgs. $14.95

Good Morning West Virginia! - Travel Guide & Recipe Collection
Features 119 recipes from 60 West Virginia inns & travel information. 160 pgs. $12.95

INDEX OF BED & BREAKFASTS